The Twisted MUSE

A COLLECTION OF POETRY AND LYRIC VERSE

RICHARD COREY

iUniverse

THE TWISTED MUSE
A COLLECTION OF POETRY AND LYRIC VERSE

iUniverse books may be ordered through booksellers or by contacting:

iUniverse
1663 Liberty Drive
Bloomington, IN 47403
www.iuniverse.com
1-800-Authors (1-800-288-4677)

ISBN: 978-1-4917-5084-1 (sc)
ISBN: 978-1-4917-5309-5 (hc)
ISBN: 978-1-4917-5085-8 (e)

Library of Congress Control Number: 2014920853

Printed in the United States of America.

iUniverse rev. date: 8/17/2015

This book is dedicated to my mother…
And a very special thanks to all the characters
That made it real and shaped my life and this book.

CONTENTS

POETRY

LYRIC VERSE

FOREWORD

By Benny R. Mills

The Twisted Muse is a title derived from a phrase that occurred as a natural part of one of many conversations I have had with the poet/author. He, like so many others, suffers from bipolar disorder, yet that very disorder sometimes provides emotional benefit, especially impetus and creative direction to artistic work. Hence, the disorder itself can become the artist's muse, albeit a twisted one. This is evident in the works of many poets, Poe being the first to mind.

As he and I worked to give structure to his ideas and emotions in both poetic and lyric form, we thought of the disorder that has apparently gifted him with such freedom to express human joy and sorrow as frequently as we thought about the actual poetry as a vehicle to express that joy and sorrow. And the poems and songs he has written do, indeed, reflect the mania and the depression that are the defining features of the disorder. In some poems, he celebrates himself as a demigod while, in others, he despairs of a demonic nature.

In that cycle of celebration and despair, we see ourselves in different cycles and periods of our own lives, for we all have experienced the joy and depression that persistently plagues those who have bipolar disorders. Ours, though, are generally situational and are spaced in time to give us the days, weeks, months, or years we need to recover. Nonetheless, we know the poet's voices and his passions, for they are our own.

And, finally, the joys and sorrows were our shared triumphs and despairs as we completed this book, fighting for words, focusing on punctuation, and formatting content to either poetry or song. Our work together has been a month, a month that passed in the clichéd blinking of an eye. It has been an exhilarating journey, and I hope the reading of this book is just so for you as well.

Now, forward to page one…

POETRY

A Note from the Author

I have lived these writings, and survived... if you aren't pleased or horrified by the first couple pages, stick with it and you will be.

R.C.

ME

I was born in a place you wouldn't know.
I was raised in a place that you'll never go.
I grew up little.
I grew up lean.
I was one of the most rotten kids you've ever seen.
I grew up rough.
I grew up tough.
I had no choice but to scar my knuckles up.
I did things to make my parents proud.
I did things to make them cuss me out loud.
I thought I was grown at sixteen,
But there were so many things I hadn't seen.
So, I left.
I went seeking fortune and fame.
Cursed and inspired by my name,
Richard Corey but with an "E".
E.A. Robinson's poem and Simon and Garfunkel's song,
Felt like a destiny, or rather a fate for me.
Yes. Just like the stories go, I tried it a couple times.
You can look at my wrists and still see the lines.
Yes. A few times. A few times when I lost my mind.
I lived up and down the east coast.
Sometimes as I aged, I felt like I was chasing Richard Cory's ghost.
Twenty years went by so fast.
I never went to sleep,
Knowing if I would wake up on the right side of the grass.
At times, I had pockets full of money.
Other times, wore hats of fame.
I even spent some time locked up,
In mental hospitals and jails with my head hung in shame.
I spent some time under the bright lights,

Making music and living plays.
Working nights… student during the days.
I found out who my friends were.
They have all been few and far between.
Some of them even tried to kill me
Others in my heart will always gleam.
Now here I am. Still lost as a man.
Lost as a poet if I actually am one.
Right or wrong.
I am just one more unfinished song.

10/5/14

A Well Painted Picture

A family picture.
Smiles turned around.
Everyone looks happy.
No one recalls the frown.
We only remember
Just what we see.
A well painted picture.
No one remembers.
No one.
No one... but me.

9/4/12

Happiness for Sale

I would give anything
to be happy every day.
But happiness has its price,
a price that I can't pay.
Not many people are happy,
for the price is way too high.
With all the money in the world,
happiness you cannot buy.
The few that are happy
must be feeling swell.
They must have had a coupon
or caught happiness on sale.

May 1989

The Gypsy Rain

Little things here and there I learned.
Forsaken lessons are for what I yearned.
My grandma looked at me in the gypsy rain
and hope showed through the layer of pain,
then gently she took me by the hand.

Out of the gypsy rain, she took me in the shack.
I knew at this point there was no turning back.
That first lesson I remember so well.
It was about tying knots and tying them like Hell,
sometimes including money, other times sand.

I could smell something rancid on the old coal stove.
Her voice echoed as the gypsy rain drove.
Consecrated jewelry she wore at all times from all lands.
Some of which still adorn my wrists and hands.
I honor my humble teacher, I viewed as a preacher.

Then back out in the gypsy rain we walked…
between the raindrops we dance and talked.
Most of my life I walked across her damp yard…
To learn tinctures, tonics, and how to read the card.
She's been gone for some time but I'm sure I can reach her.

7/26/14

ALL OF THE ABOVE

Sometimes, I am alone
in a world by myself.
No one understands me;
No one seems to help.

But in my world are other people,
which makes it nice to visit.
I know these people are merely part of me,
but which part is it?

There are many different sides to me,
and these people play the part.
Most of them are missing
because I feel torn apart.

I need a ticket out of here,
out of this lonesome land.
I know that you are hiding one,
but hiding it in which hand?

In the right, you have happiness.
In the left, you have love.
Why must I choose?
Why can't I have all of the above?

MAY, 1989

The Place that Time Forgot

Every now and then,
I'll travel an hour or two
to a place I still call home
down the winding roads of Rt. 52.

My home is close now
but still so far away.
Behind a truck filled with coal,
the short trip could last all day.

Up and down and through the mountains,
I pass a tiny green and white sign.
It marks the entrance to another world,
another time, yet only a county line.

Through all the tiny coal stained towns,
now abandoned and left in despair,
windows all broken, streets destroyed,
cities beyond repair.

As I pass through them,
each and every one,
I can still see the streets filled with people,
spending hard earned money and having fun.

Coal towns, they were called back then,
stand in shambles between me and my mountain home.
Only ghost towns now left in ruin.
How could times have gone so wrong?

Coal camps now
on my left and right.
With no one stirring, no one working, no children playing,
whether it be day or night.

On into the mountains I travel,
I finally make it there.
Up onto the hilltop where I was raised,
I stand and breathe in the coal dusted air.

I reflect on the trip I made,
which I have made many times before.
A trip I thought I'd never take again
or at least, as a younger man, I swore.

That same trip that I made to get home
was, would, and still is my way out.
Only now I'm headed in a different direction
to McDowell County, the place that time forget about.

4/14/04

OLD DOC GULLET'S PLACE

The smell of homemade wine
politely fills the air.
The sound of bluegrass music
could easily lead you there.
The old gravel road
that runs along the track
leads to Old Doc Gullet's place,
His little two room shack.
Hotter than hell in the summer time.
Colder than an abandoned mine in the winter.
His homemade wine kept him cool,
kept warm by his temper.
I would go with my dad when I was a boy
to cut the old man's hair.
I go back time to time to see his place,
but old Doc Gullett isn't there.

4/15/05

The Walker

I used to have a crutch.
I bought it by the pint.
It made this broken boy
stand up straight, like a giant.

I threw it down one day
to walk it on my own.
I thought I could do it.
I guess I was wrong.

10/27/07

My Woods

Life is a tangled wood,
Where we all get lost once or twice.
Trapped in brier thickets and stuck crossing rapid streams,
Burdens by our own device.
Scratching, scraping, clawing to the tops of hills
To tumble back down in the valley.
Once again, it's all uphill.
Your skin peeling, your face being lashed
By branches and thorns at every turn,
You never seem to find your way with one eye weeping,
Despite the short-cuts and directions that you learn.
Sometimes, I'd like to leave these woods,
Maybe even the earth just to get away.
Leave these woods and worries thereof
And possibly try again some other day.

4/12/01

THUNDERSTORM

The thunder angrily grumbles
as it tumbles through the valley of our discontent.
The rain bleeds from the clouds
and stains the ground in painful torment.
Rivers rage, the winds whip
in a twisted tango, a devilish partnership.
Lightning lights the sky.
blinds the mind's eye, the stars go out,
lost in confusion,
a brief intrusion, leaving us all in a storm of doubt.
The air freshens, teaching lessons
of war and rage, the price to pay for your possessions.
What does not wash away is lost,
For that's the cost of our sin.
What is not lost is washed away.
What was never will be again.

5/14/10

Rainbows

A rainbow is a thing of beauty, a joy forever.
The sky is on fire,
burning bright with majestic colors.
Blues and reds and oranges and yellows and greens.
setting the sky ablaze with the violets of a royal promise.
The rain soothing, raging, or simply a drizzle,
sets the sky on fire with a heavenly bow.
Most certainly, no pot of gold lies at the end of the rainbow.
But the beauty of rainbows
is worth more than all the gold any pot can hold.
So please let it pour followed by more golden sun
to set the sky on fire with color, love, passion, and promise.

4/13/11

FAITH

I put my faith in Heaven
but fell right through the clouds.
I put my faith in people
but I only parted the crowds.
I put my faith in music
but I must've played too loud.
I put my faith in you my dear
but you were far too proud.
I put my faith in you my love
but I couldn't see through your shroud.
I put my faith in you, yeah you,
and you, I let you down.

8/10/14

My Amazing Grace

Ever since I was a boy,
I looked for something with blind faith
The promise of forgiveness
The promise of Amazing Grace.

I looked in churches.
I looked in steeples.
I looked in books.
I looked in people.

I dabbled in the dark stuff
The dark magic
The dark whiskey
But it all turned out so tragic.

I almost lost my mind
when I was 22.
Almost lost my right arm
Kidneys too.

People came and prayed
While I just laid
Nearly 40 nights
39 days.

But I still didn't stop searching
more books, more gods
Hoodoo, Voodoo, things that witches do
No, I didn't like my odds.

I danced in the rain naked.
I danced between the graves.

Then all at once with my ear to a rock,
in the middle of a creek, in the middle of the day . . .
I found my Amazing Grace.

7/29/14

The Memories You Made

You haunt my heart like an angel passing out love to those who understand what the angel is doing and understand the angel's part.

My recollection and dreams are conquered and held captive by the look of love lost in those beautiful dark brown eyes.

My mind and all the random knowledge rolling and banging around in my brain are stopped instantly by songs and sonnets that sing to me and swirl around my brain in their place.

But most of all the memories you made of how you kiss, how you smell, and how you hold me are still felt every night just as boldly as if you were here.

But then as tears start to stain my pillows and I lose you in my mind, I just feel lost, alone, with such little faith that you will ask me to come home.

I just want to hear those words one day.

"Baby, please come home."

10/26/12

MY BROKEN ANGEL

I often wondered what brought you into my life.
Perhaps you were an angel flying too close to the ground.
You had the wings to prove it,
But I didn't see a halo.
Maybe you just didn't want to use it.
You were standing so close to me I caught your scent,
a mixture of roses and honeysuckle.
You were definitely Heaven sent.
Closer and closer we grew,
everyday something new.
You had quite the appetite for everything I loved.
It was as if we were the same person
or at least close enough.
Sent to me.
Meant for me.
But we never gained custody of what was supposed to be.
Life tore us apart.
And we just let it. Afraid to speak,
Afraid to mention what was in our heart,
Our lips too tight to let the truth leak.
I can still smell the roses and honeysuckle,
Though you're so far away from me.
Without you all my roses have faded to black.
If only your broken wings could bring you back.

7/9/12

Queen of Hearts

I've never been a lucky man,
always dealt the worst of hands,
never had a handful of aces,
or a matching set of smiling faces.

Until now, the queen of diamonds
was the best I could do,
a useless card,
a card meant to make men blue.

But, perhaps, I have been playing the wrong game,
a game of sorrow,
a game of pain.

Maybe, I shouldn't be playing at all.
A full house, a royal flush,
they're all useless,
one and all.

I don't need four of a kind.
I've already won. It's in the charts.
I only need you,
My queen of hearts.

2/6/11

First Love

Sometimes I wished I was a kid again,
around sixteen or seventeen.
Perhaps, I should explain what I mean.
Everything was new
driving, dating,
and including my love for you.
I remember the feeling in my chest,
the lack of rest, and being scared to death.
The look in your in your eyes was such a surprise.
I knew that you felt it too.
Oh, those few days,
I was so amazed.
I couldn't get enough of you
but I lost you for a while.
A couple years later, though I couldn't believe it.
I saw that smile.
I never thought I'd get to see it again.
There you were...my love, my friend.
My childhood love was back.
So happy you made me.
Even though only 3 years it would last,
3 years so fast.
But even today,
you're so far away,
you manage to make me smile.
I feel so old most of the time
but when I hear your voice,
see your face, see you smile.
I feel the love, I felt as a child.

8/26/14

December

Hello.
It's clear to see
that you don't recognize me.
I know
it's been a long, long while.
And I have forgotten how to smile.
But would that help you to remember?
All we had was that December.
The yellow Christmas rose
I placed behind you ear.
And I left. Yes, I left.
I left out of fear
so long ago.
I won't bother you again.
I don't want to scare you.
I just want to be your friend.
But would that help you to remember?
All we had was that December.
The Christmas rose I placed behind your ear.
And I left. No, I ran
out of fear.

12/12/12

WHERE WILL WE GO

Where will we go? I don't know.
But wherever it is, I'm sure love will follow.
A cruise to nowhere, a flight to heaven,
Or a trip to bed from seven to seven.
Anywhere with you is where I want to be.
No price is too high, regardless of your fee.
Swim with the dolphins, dance with the stars,
Love under the moon, float in the ocean, sharing one heart.
Perhaps a train, possibly a plane,
I would walk to the end of the earth across coals of flame.
Where would you like to go?
Somewhere warm or somewhere with snow?
Hot or cold, I would keep you warm or cool.
Be your prince, be your fool.
The beauty of Jamaica. The love in Rome.
Regardless of where we will go,
With you, I'll be home.

4/11/11

When You Are Not Around

Oh, how I miss you
and long to kiss you.
I still recall the taste of your lips.
I'm counting down the days
until I can see your face.
Your arms around my neck, mine around your hips.
Oh, how long can I go?
Time, it moves so slow
when you are not around.
It's like waiting for a train to cross the tracks.
It goes so slow until you come back.
Then, the hands on the clock just spin 'round.
There will never be enough time
for you to be mine,
not enough hours in the day,
not enough days in the week,
No grass growing beneath our feet.
Stitching up so much time God would be amazed.
So whatever time may bring,
It won't matter I've got enough string.

9/7/12

Anything for You

I would strike a million match sticks just to see the flames.
Pick them up and build a house just to put flowers in the window
panes.
It may sound tedious,
a little absurd.
It may sound ridiculous,
something that is unheard.
But that's what I'd do.
Yeah, that's what I'd do
just to spend one more hour with you.

I would walk across the ocean, but I wouldn't sink.
Lay upon the Dead Sea,
the salty water I would drink.
It may sound ludicrous.
It can't be done.
I may sound crazy,
damaged by the sun.
But that's what I'd do.
Yeah, that's what I'd do
just to spend one more minute with you.

I know I'm merely mortal.
I know I'm a bit insane.
You are the stars in my sky.
You are my refreshing rain.
I would walk to the end of each rainbow.
I would paint the sky a new blue.
I would steal an angel's halo.
Anything for you.

I would hike the Himalayas,
no shoes upon my feet.
I would sleep on a glacier,
dreams of you my only heat.
It may sound silly,
maybe I'm a little cracked.
It may sound extreme, but baby it's a fact.
That's what I'd do.
Yeah, that's what I'd do
just to spend one more second with you.

Yeah, that's what I'd do,
anything for you.
That's what I'd do
just to catch one last glimpse of you.

9/13/04

Longing for the Day Lily

Those words they are so sweet:
"A thousand kisses deep."
Forever I will wait
Destiny, Happenstance, or Fate
To hold you around the waist
Sway...We will sway.
Whisk the night away.
A dime a dance they say.
A diamond chance my play.
You think I want nothing
but I want it all.
In the summer or in the fall...
...Flowers float from Heaven to litter your path.
From now until then...From then until now
Everyday without the math.
It's just you in my mind
All the time
You and me
Some tequila and lime
Quite the combination
I'd say the least.
Do you really want me?
Can you really tame this beast?
Between your legs is Heaven
I am not at all afraid to say
Because I've always found safety there
In your arms I want to stay.
Taste the dew upon your lily
For the taste of you has never left my mind.
Your lips they are so supple.
Your neck tastes so sweet.

Every inch of you from your head to your feet
This will surely destroy me
My undoing…My defeat.
To you I surrender
My heart and soul
My spirit, my being
For you love,
Everything…Every part of me
Completely belongs to you forever.
The world will slip away,
When we are finally returned
Back together.

10/7/14

All I'll Ever Need

I cross my heart,
And I swear:
I'll always be there for you.

If you could only see
how much you mean to me.
Till then, these words will have to do.

Thick, thin, or flush.
Just the thought of your touch
On my cheek.
You love is all I'll ever need.

A pinky swear or bible oath,
Either one or maybe both -
I'll pledge my love to you.

A good morning kiss,
Or a kiss goodnight
By the moon or candlelight.

Angel or devil,
I don't care.
By your side, I'll be there.
Your breath warm and sweet,
Your love is all I ever need.

A day dream
Or in real life;
As long as you'll be my wife.

The love that you give me
Will always be with me.
Just whisper it softly,
Just as you breathe.

Your love is all I'll ever need.

You are all I'll ever need.

9/26/11

THE LOVER AND THE LONG HANDED JOURNAL

Oh, Lord! Oh, Lord!
In his little black book,
the country Don Juan
records his success.
A soft, gentle kiss,
a hand up a dress.
He cannot miss
soft moans in his ear,
nor the firm flesh
of her ample rear.
Her shuddering moistness
he holds so dear!
Oh, dear! Oh, dear!

Oh, my! Oh, my!
In a hard bound book
of velvet - soft, luxurious,
and green -
the poet's firm hand
marks stiff,
sharp, and keen.
Self-induced stains
long wiped clean.
The wet black ink
of a poet's lonely dream.
Trapped among sticky pages,
sticky words begin to stink.
Prudish publishers reject him,

and a poet's heart and his pen
sink.
Oh, no! Oh, no!

10/24/07

THE RING

Awaiting your phone call
is like awaiting your next breath.
For if it doesn't come soon enough,
you must surely face your death.

But when that telephone jingles
and it's you on the other end,
my heart, my love, my life,
my one and only, my lover, my friend.

And with a simple hello,
the heavens open and the angels sing
the most beautiful sound,
awakened by a simple ring.

2/6/11

CHRISTMAS TO ME

Christmas to me?
Well, there has to be a tree.
A real tree, one that lived,
one that at one point was free.
Lights will be strung,
Ornaments hung one by one.
All this done just for fun.
A background of Christmas melodies,
soft and low.
The lights begin to glow.
Presents and stockings,
skirts on trees,
isn't that shocking?
Perhaps, the jingle bells will be rocking.
And, since there really is no place to go,
I really do wish it would snow.
We could cuddle up
under a blanket of fleece.
Candles flicker,
giving us peace.
You.
Me.
Alone in a winter wonderland
Reality, not TV.
Happy Christmas To Me!

12/24/07

Fade and Time

Winter, Summer, Spring, Fall.
As the seasons pass,
we must suffer them all.
People, Animals, Fish, Plants.
All at the world's command,
we must dance.
It goes unnoticed, tragic,
as if the world suffers
from an evil witch's magic.
We rise with the spring,
Ambitious and full of courage,
ready for anything the summer may bring.
We stand strong to worship the sun,
but as the summer beats us down
until it's no longer fun.
In the fall. we do as the name suggests,
falling just like the leaves
but giving time our best.
As our hair and the ground show,
Winter brings the snow.
Too tired to do it all again,
not even one last show.
The saddest part played,
despite the Earth's infinite power,
is the fading…the fading of that last precious flower.

10/2/12

The Duality of a Heart

You make me want to live.
You make me want to die.
You make me want to smile.
You make me want to cry.
You make me want to look around.
You make me want to fall back.
You make me feel safe.
You make me feel like I'm under attack.
You make my heart flutter.
You make my heart break.
You make me feel so confident.
You make me feel as if I am a mistake.
You make me want to hold you.
You make me want to run away.
You have such calming words...
You make me so afraid.
You make me feel so alive.
You make me feel so dead.
You make me want to take back the world.
You make want to live only in my head.
Such simple logic but so hard to understand...
...with such ease, dear, you create the duality of man.

10/04/13

THE PART YOU THROW AWAY

I usually don't have a problem
finding the right words to write.
They come to me at dawn.
They come to me moonlight.
Putting them together . . .
that's the prickly part.
Noun. Verb. Conjunction. Adjective.
Do they come from the brain or the heart?
I guess that depends
on who your audience will be.
A publisher, a magazine,
a lover or just me.
I've been told by family and friends,
"You're not a poet. You're just a prick with a pen."
I usually don't believe them
or the things they say.
But at other times,
I feel like the bruised part of a strange fruit
you simply throw away.

8/27/14

PASSIONATE PAUSES

Well penned passion
printed on parchment of white.
No "t" or "i" left unfinished.
It seems too wrong to be right.
Paper aged and yellowed,
too old to be written
as early as last night.
Too powerful and moving
to be written with even a hint of fright.
No place for pauses.
Poisonous pen work.
Not too passive or perfect.
Not too deep but not at all trite.
Pockets filled with posies.
Perfumed for the masses.
Perfectly pushed through the classes,
like an arrow takes flight.
Keeping lips pursed and parted,
as if persuaded by sirens.
Pentacles and Pentagrams
painted by Picasso on Pandora's box.
Well penned passion for pennies
passes for love on the past hands of all the clocks of the world.
Tick, tock, tick, tock…tick.

6/13/13

THE QUIET MAN

I hold it all inside
Like a balloon ready to pop.
But I am afraid if I let any of it out,
I won't be able to stop.
It's a tough life to live this way,
But I have done it for years.
Punching on trees, running for miles,
And finding safe, silent places to shed some tears.
Still silent, still afraid, still strong
Screaming inside, filled with courage, still wrong.
Some things, small and large, some things need to be said,
Some heard, and some read.
I have the ability to speak and the ability to write.
Maybe, I've gotten more patient over the years
Or just maybe I'm too old to fight.
Sometimes, you find yourself simply at a loss of words,
Even me, when you've listened to something that can't be unheard.
Should I fight, cry, laugh, or continue to hold it in,
Hold it in as long as I can?
And continue to be the quiet man.

3/11/13

WHY?

I don't want to live,
Yet I don't want to die.
I always seem confused.
I always wonder why.
Why are we living?
No one can really tell.
Why is here a heaven?
Why is here a hell?
Why must we die?
I don't really know.
I just want to leave,
But I don't know where to go.
Why is the question,
For there is no real reply.
No matter what we do,
We will always wonder why.

JUNE, 1991

THE BASTARD SON

I've never written in a voice quite this high.
Perhaps, it's because I know my voice simply won't fly.
When I think of you, I think of the angels,
How high they are perched in heaven,
And smile down on you and ring their bells.

Because you're their sister,
You've no need to address God as mister.
For he is your father,
And you are the Chosen One
By God and the angels.
And me? I am the bastard son.

I know I don't deserve you.
The Lord has perfectly preserved you
For someone much better than me,
But maybe, just maybe,
The Lord will save me
And give me a chance to be with you.

Here are we, the connected three:
Your heavenly father,
God's only daughter,
The Chosen One
By God and the angels,
And me, the bastard son.

But why? Oh why
Must I be denied
The only thing I've wanted in life?
Battered and beaten!

Denied of my freedom!
Why can't the all-seeing see
You were meant for me?

I will beg, barter, plead,
Just to be heard as I cry
Because you are so special,
A heavenly angel,
The reasons for rainbows
And tears in your heavenly father's eyes.

I may be the bastard son,
But for you I wish to be the Only One.
It's God's heart or mine
That will be broken in time.
Illegitimate and lost and blue!
God knows our love is worth
All the riches on earth.
While you belong to God,
I forever remain yours,
The bastard son.

12/25/12

THE ANGRY CLOWN

I am not a poet.
Even I know it.
With my make-up painted on upside down,
I am nothing more than an angry clown.
I have just a few words to right.
Perhaps I should just shut my mouth and be quiet.
Who wants to hear what I have to say?
They're just ramblings from a madman anyway.
Even my bi-polar brain can't sort through it,
All the rhymes and bullshit.
I can't be a star anymore.
Don't want to anyway.
Now I'm just an ink pen whore.
Who knows what will come through my parted lips?
Maybe I took just one too many psychotic trips.
I never made it back.
Now, my soul is black.
No, Ma I ain't drinking.
And I ain't on the pot.
My crippled brain has simply begun to rot.
I don't want to live.
I don't want to die.
Willing to give all I have
to those in the sky.
But who knows, maybe that's a lie.
I'm not a liar.
I'm not a thief.
I'm just a clown full of grief.
Always guilty.
Never free.
Get these fucking demons out of me.

They're sucking me dry from the inside out.
Instruments I can't play.
Songs I can't sing.
Not too far from purgatory.
I hope you have enjoyed my story.
Every word.
Every line.
Every sentence.
Every rhyme.
A twisted writer,
with a twisted view.
Twisted words,
from the twisted muse.
Pick me up.
Lift me up to the top of my funeral pyre.
Use rum to start the fire.
Let it burn to the ground.
Say goodbye to the angry clown.

06/05/13

CRY, CRY, CRY

Cry, Cry, Cry.
Bitch, whine, and complain.
Take more pills,
To dull the pain.
Prescribe me this.
Prescribe me that.
Feed me more.
Make me fat.
Push, pull, and tug
To and fro.
Sweep me under the rug.
Shake me up,
So you can watch me glow.
No more glitter,
No more shine.
I've become more dull,
With the passing of time.
Sparkle, glitter, and fade.
Hey, devil, I've got a soul to trade.
A soul to sell for you to buy.
I'm going cheap.
No more use for me.
Just cry, cry, cry.

12/27/07

Smiling At My Life

I smile at the demons
that live under my bed.
I smile when the pain comes . . .
the pain inside my head.
I swallow rattlesnakes.
I swallow them whole.
So they can poison the evil
deep inside my soul.
I sleep with the devil
beside me in this bed.
Him with his pitchfork . . .
me with my six pieces of lead.
I smile at trouble.
I smile at you.
I smile at the sky
just because it's blue.
Blue like the diamonds
hiding in your eyes.
Blue like Coltrane . . .
don't look surprised.
I smile at news radio
because none of it's new.
I've lived it all
in my first life with you.
Crossroads and double-crosses.
Crucifixes too.
I don't trust Jesus,
peace lovin' hippie Jew.
Trust is an issue
between me and all my Gods.
Ones that live in the sky,

even inside myself . . .
you must applaud.
I can't trust the broken heart
that beats inside my chest.
I can't trust my own thoughts.
I can't get no rest.
All I want is one more thrill.
Only one decision,
who else am I gonna kill?
Up close and personal,
I want more blood on my hands.
The body I will toss.
Then get the fuck outta my way . . .
it's my turn on the cross.
It's my turn now . . .
too bad Jew.
Back to the desert,
I'll use your nails
and smile at you too.

8/14/14

Two Bit...None the Richard

On my deathbed
In an interstate motel room,
I hear
the eternal zoom of the highway
and - walls - so thin
too many conversations drifting in.
I cannot determine
hallucination from realization.
My hands shake, with minor tambourine trembles
as I try to pray.
Lights passing by so white,
disguise night from day.
I long for lover
to pull stained sheets over my eyes.
So afraid to sleep,
I don't know if I will live or die.
In every single turn of the corridors of my mind
lurk memories of the good and bad, the rich and poor.
Have I lived a dream or simply opened the wrong door?
Lying here with my graveyard tan,
Tombstone eyes,
Dirt on my knees
from where I knelt to cry.
A needle, nose down, skin popping through,
maybe a card or a flower or two,
and dozen white roses laid out on my grave.
If I could,
"Thank You" is what I'd say.
I know it's over;
I'm found to be a fraud,
last breath begging to half-deaf God.

I know it's over.
Freedom songs are all I've ever had,
just a part of me
that I guess ain't all been bad.
If you can't afford it, check my pocket
I'll need two bits...
I'm sure I got it.

4/14/14

KINGDOM OF HEAVEN

Some may call me blasphemous,
but I assure you what they say is true.
Most think Heaven is somewhere in the clouds,
up there in great big blue.
Do you really believe that?
Do you?
Do you honestly think we're gonna hang out
in the clouds singing praying and watching re-runs of Touched
By An Angel
while we drink wine and eat bread and get fat and get fat and
get fat?
I'm sorry friend that's not how it is; it don't work like that.
Living in the clouds is simply untrue
Because the Kingdom of Heaven is inside of you.
Inside of you.
Inside of you.

4/11/12

Let Loose of the Strings

Is this the way life is supposed to go?
Just taking us down, blow by blow?
If it is Lord, I'm out. You win.
Can't you feel me tapping out again and again?

You've got the best of me. Let me go.
Send me to Hell or give me a halo.
Either is better than this daily grind.
You already know. You know I've lost my mind.

Did you have a hand in that or no?
You promised never to lay on us that kind of load.
Pills in the morning. Pills at night.
Pills for everything. How in the hell is that right?

Your choice or free choice? How do we know?
If you're pulling the strings, I hope you enjoy the show.
I imagine you've got your DVR set for mine.
Probably wouldn't want to miss an episode where I beg and stand
in line.

Stand in line for forgiveness. Stand in line to lose my sorrow.
Oops, you're not in today. Guess I'll be back tomorrow.
Or maybe not, I'm tired of this eternal role.
Fuck it! It's just my soul.

9/28/12

TRUST

Trust is a word so lightly used.
It should be removed from our vocabulary.
Trust me. Trust what you see.
Can you believe? Oh, quite the contrary.
What is real? What we can feel?
Although what we can feel sometimes is altered,
Make believe, created by our hearts and minds
And is only what we perceive.

1/1/05

The Extermination of Freedom

Sure, they may beat me into the ground,
but they'll never keep me down!
I will rise, rise, rise from the ashes like the fiery phoenix!
On its burning wings, I'll soar into flight,
blazing a trail of freedom into the darkest of night.

Sure, the freedom of expression
and the freedom of speech
have long been extinguished
by politicians and priests,
long winded, loud spouting,
whispering and shouting
about what is wrong and what is right,
and we fall for these back door politics
from false prophets and heretics,
all fueled by power and greed,
only concerned in amassing more money
than their fat fucking asses can bleed.

Sure, I could be wrong,
but haven't we all heard the end to this sad song?
They will come for my head
calling me Red
until they are sure I am dead
for the things I have said.
Let them throw the first stones, they without sin!
They can silence me like all the others,
but in blood or ink they can't silence the pen of my brothers!

8/28/11

THE MINDLESS RAMBLINGS
OF A MAD MAN

Who listens to the mindless ramblings of a mad man?
The masses? The youth? The church?
When is it necessary for me to make my decision
of whether or not I choose to be God or the Antichrist?
It's all just a position of power. Right?
Who will follow me?
Where will I take them?
When the snow melts, is it Spring?
Do you mind if I wake you up for the
end of the world?
I wouldn't want you to miss it.
Will you scream when you die?
You screamed when you were born.
Is birth the beginning of life or death?
Life is nasty, brutish, and short.
Who said that?
I said that. Weren't you listening?
No. Originally? Thomas Hobbes.
A philosopher, a dreamer, a drunk.
Who listens to the mindless ramblings of a mad man?
All.

04/04/08

I Dare You

I dare you to dare me.
I dare you to take control.
I dare you to wrestle
with the remnants of my soul.
I dare you to be the hero
or, better yet, assume the villain's role.
I dare you to take my life
or try to make me whole.
I dare you to take a walk
on the path that leads through my mind.
I dare you to keep up.
I dare you to fall behind.
I dare you to daydream,
daydream inside my thoughts.
I feel sorry for you
if you get lost.
So hang on to my coat tails.
Don't dare let go.
I'll take you for a ride
and leave you to hitchhike to make it home.
I dare you to enter the house
when you know you're there alone.
Who knows what you'll walk in on,
a sacrifice on a moonless night, a black cat bone.
It is all false or true?
Go find out. I dare you. I double dare you.

2/20/11

A Musical Word for the Night

Every night I wonder and I ponder
about ways to make music with only one word.
How can I make the silence of a deadened night
come alive, yet remain unheard?

What word could I use:
stillness, peace, placidity, tranquility?
There are so many words from which to choose.
I simply am not sure any of these are just.
What about the things that fill the night:
the sounds of night birds or the animal sounds of lust?
Would this night fall on a city full of empty sound
or in the wilderness with only the wind and me around?

Or how about Spring, alive with the sound of life?
But I can't focus on the sunshine or the rainbows,
Because I am still drawn back to that silent night.
In the Winter, it is so quiet I can hear the snowfall,
but that is still not the melody.
Perhaps the word I am searching for is just a little off key.
In the Summer, the fireflies will guide the path of my pen.

I'm still searching for that perfect note
to bring this poem to an end.
Am I not talented enough?
Is my writing not that keen?
The sound I long to hear must be musical enough to describe the
scene serene.

What is the word I seek to describe the music of the night?
Where can I look to find the word for the music of the moon
hanging round?
It is the music of the quiet of the night, the silence of sound.

7/6/11

THE FLY

Who killed the fly?
It was not I.
So why must I cry?
It was only a fly.
But why?
Why did the fly have to die?
Did it land on your pie?
Or perhaps, it flew into someone's eye.
Maybe, we will never know why?
Things die.
It was only a fly.
So don't you cry.
The burden will lie
if only with I.
It was only a fly.
It was just a fly.

9/28/11

BEHIND THE SMILES AND MIRRORS

When I woke up this morning,
my life was a silent movie
playing on a black and white wall.
An old time Kodak projector,
flickering and flashing
No pause or stop on these old machines.

We just have to watch what plays,
the scenes of shattered dreams.
No way to stop the projector. We just can't turn it off.
We can beg please,
but we can't turn off memories.

So much pain. So much despair.
Head in our hands,
and running fingers through our hair,
Gray before our time.
Never could we toe the mark; never could we walk the line.

All I ever wanted was a little sunshine in the rain.
A chance to smile.
Smiling to hide the pain.
A smile is a mask,
A mask to hide the monster that lives inside.
So hard to keep it hidden,
behind a mask and a plastic smile.

Who puts the pressure on? God or Satan?
Could you let up for just a little while?
I just want to breathe,
inhale and exhale,

without all this pressure on my chest.
Just one day to feel well.
The mental madness you've laid on me
is like an web of tangled snakes in my head.
I don't even want to be "normal".
The way I used to be would be fine
even though the life I led was never really mine.
Do this. Do that. Take orders. Forget facts.
Do as I tell you, not as I do.
Well, fuck that. Who the hell are you?

Pressure. Pressure. Pressure.
I can't take it anymore.
It's an absolute crying shame
when there are parts of my brain
that I'm afraid to explore.
Some things are better left forgotten,
although you wear them all over your face.
I can't run. I can't hide.
Funhouse mirrors are all over the place.

10/13/12

Writer's Block

Nothing is coming to mind.
I reach into the depths of my brain
to see what I find.
Nope. Nothing there. No use.
Perhaps I should brush my teeth or polish my shoes --
No, wait! Wait! I got it! I got it...Damn, there it goes.
Well, I could stand to wash a load of clothes.
Maybe vacuum....No, something has to come soon.
I guess I'll get a rag and just dust the room.
No, no, no. I want to write.
Politics, maybe?
Ahhh hell, I don't want to watch the news tonight.
Religion? Naaaaa...it's been done.
Sex? Well, now, that could be fun!
Where should I start though?
Definitely with a woman! But where would I go?
I guess sex is too dirty.
It positively is if I write about my life before thirty.
Okay, okay. Think. Think.
Maybe it would help if I had a drink.
Well, it couldn't hurt.
Now, I've had three, so let's get to work . . .
Damn! I think I'm drunk!
What about love and that Pepe whatever...you know, the stalker
skunk?
Well, shit!
Writer's block?
Aha, that's it!

10/9/11

What is a Writer?

What is a writer?
One who simply writes lines?
Or is he the artist,
who creates images and thoughts in the mind?

Are you really a writer
if no one reads your work?
All the greats weren't recognized
until they were covered with dirt.

Will that be my fate?
Will I never be heard?
I have too much to say.
I'm sorry if it makes you unnerved.

It's easy to describe a butterfly.
You can see it. It's real.
The beauty is in creating the wind from its wings,
fluttering on your face and how that must feel.

It is sad that life leads to death,
Sad but true.
I know you don't want to imagine it,
but it is coming for me and for you.

Sadness doesn't make me happy.
Death will not set me free.
But the pain doesn't hurt so bad
when you're not afraid to discuss it openly.

Too rash. Too proud. Too difficult.
I guess I am.

Too passionate. Too cynical. Too truthful.
Follow me if you can.

What was pleasant about Poe?
What was pleasant about Plath?
What was pleasant about Jim Morrison
dying in his bath?

Does that take away from their art?
Van Gogh cut off his own ear
because the Devil supposedly spoke to him.
And it's my thoughts that you fear?

Shunned by the different
because my writing is too strange.
"We support freedom of expression."
But only if it fits into our frame.

I say, break the frame!
Rip it apart!
It's not right to fill a frame
if the frame surrounds no art.

But what do I know?
I'm just some crazy man.
But if you took the time to know me,
you may be my biggest fan.

I simply don't fit in.
This world is just too picky.
But, so am I.
Now, ain't this web real sticky?

At one time, I was so strong,
such a fighter.
Now I'm old, confidence gone,
too strange to be a writer.

I guess I could write for Hallmark.
Happy, touchy drivel.
But if that's what being a writer is
I will gladly just scribble.

04/04/08

The Evil Inside of Me

When I close my weary eyes,
I drift in a cloud of voodoo smoke.
A brown island priestess disrobes
And enters a bath of watery blood
And soaks, while chanting and spewing
Puerto Rican rum and blood of the chicken
She chokes.

A Crow medicine man rocks and chants
And tries to sweat this darkness out of me.
Maybe, he went blind; maybe, he simply can't see.
The evil that lives inside of me
Burns his black eyes red
While he calls upon the white horse
To deliver the rattling bones of the dead.

Shamans and voodoo priests have failed me.
I don't know who could help me.
Or who would be willing.
The things that spew from me,
The things that I think,
The things that I write,
The things that I do,
aren't meant to hurt any of you,
But sometimes they speak of killing.

Take heed, take heed, hark, and listen:
The vanities of this world turn on a dime.
Not only gold but also I may glisten.
I used to glitter, sparkle, and shine.
That was before I completely lost my mind.

Pray. Chant. Curse.
Go ahead. You only make it worse.
Who can I blame?
The bitch that bore me
Or the bastard that lied to me?
And he still does to this day,
As if the truth would 'cause the world to burst.

My heart is lump of coal
in a diamond mine.
No one will pick me up.
No one will consider me a find.
Kicked out of the way,
Left to rot.
My sparkle is gone.
My heart is a rock.

11/17/13

Polaroid Paranoia

Have you ever felt someone spying on you?
You get lost and their camera finds you.
It catches you from a different point of view,
an angle your mirror hides from you.

You can't see it.
You never find it.
Look as you may.
Look as you will.
A stalker. A lover.
A fan. A brother.
Still photography is a skill.
And look. A look?
One look can kill.

A thousand words, our pictures are wasted.
So close, this new perspective, you can taste it.
Lip to lip, a cinnamon kiss from a demon.
You can't wake up because you're not dreaming.

At the crossroads, you stand before an old iron gate,
just before the stroke of midnight. It's not too late.
Left, right, or straight? In or out?
You choose your views, free will, filled with doubt.

Direction.
You can't see it.
You never find it.
Wading through
waist deep shit.
An angel, the Devil

black moon, never level.
Suck it in, pierce your skin.
Believe it, perceive it.
A view, you can't see it.
Still photography is a skill.
And look. A look?
One look can kill.

If you dare to peek, to peer, even to glance,
don't look back! There's no second chance.
No need for cash at a boney dance,
where skeletons there wear no pants.

You're merry, a ferry.
Your cross, you carry.
Don't look, no Book.
They see you coming.
The Devil's drumming...

You've looked. You're hooked.
Done deal. Blood seal.

Graveyard photography is a skill.
One look can kill.

4/29/14

THEY

Sometimes they cry.
Sometimes they scream.
Sometimes, they speak in dreams.

Sometimes they beg.
Sometimes they plead.
Sometimes, they speak of need.

Sometimes they whisper.
Sometimes they shout.
Sometimes, they try to get out.

Sometimes they linger.
Sometimes they share.
Sometimes, they fight for air.

Sometimes they lie.
Sometimes they're honest.
Sometimes, they sneak up on us.

Sometimes they're in a crowd.
Sometimes they're all alone.
Sometimes, they moan and groan.

Sometimes they are silent.
Sometimes they are jumbled.
Sometimes, they mumble.

Sometimes they are dirty.
Sometimes they are clean.
Sometimes, they do the unforeseen.

Sometimes they are forceful.
Sometimes they haunt.
Sometimes, they just tell me what they want.

Sometimes I ignore them.
Sometimes I listen.
Sometimes, I lose my position.

Sometimes they are here.
Sometimes they are gone.
Sometimes, they won't leave me alone.

Sometimes they scare me.
Sometimes they demand.
Sometimes, they force my hand.

Sometimes they rise from the bottom.
Sometimes they sink from the top.
Lately though, they never, never, never stop.

04/03/08

The Bowl of Souls Is Empty

People often ask me
how it feels to be the boy with no soul.
And I reply, "Why, it's much
like being the last guy with all the gold."

A soul is a bargaining chip,
a ticket for the last ship;
glimmering, glistening, sparkling, ministering.
A drop, a drip, a drink, a sip;
speaking in tongues, hands on my hips.

Where did it go?
Was it just a shadow?
Never there, none to share, a pocket full of air?
Where the wind blows, out the window, there it goes;
where it lands, no one ever knows.

I checked my pockets. I checked my brain.
All I know is I am going insane.
Hand over hand., digging in the sand,
I came to learn, to understand.

With no soul, eyes don't glow.
A witch in hand, buried in the snow.
A bus, a train,
the horns don't blow.

The thunder rolls.
The lightning crashes.
I try to steal all the souls.
The demon at the crossroads with my spirit clashes.

I need at least one soul
to offer the devil when she comes.
She'll be here soon,
too late to run.

Shackled to my grandmother's headstone,
surrounded by the witches, the bitches,
the Devil's snitches, alone,
beaten down by my grandmother's bones.

Please leave me alone.
I have no soul.
Can't you smell the empty shell,
just skin and bones?

The moon arises,
the wraith surprises,
the Devil takes my hand.

Leave this man alone,
with gypsy bones.
He is mine and mine alone.

My son, my slave,
his emptiness I crave.
Before the sun arises, you shall all find surprises.
The last, the past, your empty days.

Take one last look in this man's eyes.
There lies the surprise.
And to you all, good day.

5/13/14

STONED SOUP

Times around here have certainly changed.

Can't afford no beer no more,

definitely not a whore.

Scripts have bee rearranged.

The faces scare me like Halloween masks.

It just ain't right.

So I bummed a light for my cigarette from the candles in the church.

And took a drink of wine from the cask.

I crumbled into a dumpster chair,

hid my eyes so I wouldn't scare.

Los dias de los muertos is some freaky shit.

No place for an acid trip.

Definitely not more than one hit.

I feel the dead crawling all over me.

I was sprawling around,

then tightened into a ball on a patch of clover trying to get free.

Free from me.

Free from the dead.

Knee deep in blood,

fighting the flood in my head.

Dancing around in a suit of my bones.

Don't shoot! Don't shoot!

This is my best suit!

Leave me the fuck alone!

Devil take these God damned souls,

or God or the ferryman or Davy Jones.

Someone must be sleeping on the job.

Jesus didn't die alone.

Who didn't eat their pie?

Let them be stoned.

This adobe mud is perfect.

Pick it up.

Pick it up and throw with all your might.

Just like a ball.

Don't miss!

Walk right over there and if you can't walk then crawl.

MMM...Licky Licky...MMM...Licky Licky.

Soup for the soul.

A big fire of desire.

MMM...Licky Licky.

Drink your soup from the blackened old skull.

It's after midnight; the day is over.

What a relief.

What!

They cooked me from the knees down.

It was my meat in the pot.

I was the only one stoned.

A tear comes to my eye.

I frown. I moan. How will I get back home?

4/14/14

THE COCK-EYED OPTIMIST AND THE UNGRACIOUS HOST

Who should we fear the most?
The cock-eyed optimist or the ungracious host?
What good is the glass to be half full
if it's given with a cold hand and is filled with bull?

Life is full of these dichotomies.
Is it better to burn or better to freeze?
Questions, questions, questions,
but never any answers.
Send in the poets, the jesters, or the dancers.

Is it entertainment only because it's on tv?
Have we forgotten how to think?
Have we forgotten how to read?
We make celebrities out of criminals,
the most out of the minimal,
gods out of generals.

We should all be pitied by the pitiful.
What good is it to have a genius IQ
if a man can't make up his mind
who to be or what to do?
Life is merely a passing, fleeting fancy.
A dog and pony show.
"Always a bridesmaid, never a burro."

What's the point?
What's the cost?
If you knew where it was,
it wouldn't be lost.

No matter where you go, you'll always be there.
Right where you left off,
sleeping in the lounge chair.

When the hammer falls,
what will really matter?
When you turn over the tables,
all the crystal will shatter.
Be careful not to step on the glass

eye of the man who foretells the past.

Passed the gates, step into the future.
The founder of the feast is a heartless butcher.

"The heart is a lonely hunter."

Use the jagged edge to slice the butter.

That side always lands face down
and it's that kind of fat that spoils the ground.
Spoiled ground bears no fruit.
But then again, there is good and bad news.
You can choose:

the ungracious host or the cock-eyed optimist's gift.

There is plenty to eat, but they only serve shit.

7/8/11

Naked Rain

I was shocked and wounded
by the things that the moon did
That Night.

I was dancing naked in the rain.

Shimmering and shining,
the rain looked liked diamonds
flying straight towards my eyes.
Lying there, I tried to catch the moon,
but it was always just out of reach.

I rolled around naked in the mud,
like a two dollar whore,
planting myself in the earth, fertilized with my fore fathers blood.
My seed was sown like a pit from a peach,
embedded in the flesh of the firmament.

And I kept staring at the moon for hours
till it started blinking secret codes
in a post-coital rhythm.
I swear I saw three or two or two or three
individually, positively, wrapped
little yellow pasteurized processed cheese products,
dancing in the sky amongst the sheets of naked rain.

Hey, diddle diddle. Hey, diddle diddle.
I didn't know how to feel or what was real.
But who gives a fuck?
I feared the rain would abruptly turn

into dripping Velveeta of my libido on my naked body,
and I didn't need a burn like that.

So I got up and jumped over the moon,
went inside my tenement on wheels not a minute too soon,
and the stars burned out leaving the lonely moon
Naked in the Rain.

7/12/12

THE CRAZIEST MAN ALIVE

I am packing my bags and heading out.
Nowhere in particular,
just down the water spout.

There will be no search party.
No rescue team.
I'll be too far gone down stream.

Don't look out the windows.
Don't you dare take a peek.
Lock your doors,
for I am the craziest man you'll ever meet.

You won't miss me once I'm bones.
You won't cry.
You'll fill my throne.

Never for me,
but you live at His feet.
'Cause I am the craziest man you'll ever beat.

Don't you dare cry.
Don't you dare lie.
Don't even try to pretend to look down the street
for the craziest man you'll ever greet.

I wouldn't hurt you.
Dare to desert you.
I seem way to meek
to be the craziest man, the looniest freak.

Crazy.
Insane.
Unhinged.
No brain.
Lost in dreams.
Dancing in streams.
A scarecrow on the yellow brick road.

Twisted.
Deranged.
Unstable.
No brain.
Tangled in weeds.
Hiding in trees.
The craziest man you'll ever see.

Am I dangerous
to myself or others?
Do I desire to slay
my father and mother?
My sister, my brother?

Turn me off
before I am set off.
I can't repay
what you've lost.

I want it all.
Prepared to take it.
Control of the world
butt ass naked.

To rule the free world,
if it truly exists,

demanding God save me
with my bloodstained fists.

Blood in the fountain,
Won't that be a treat? Don't you think?
I'm the craziest man to take a drink.

I dance around nuts
removing my guts.
Intestines lay at my feet,
the feet of the craziest man you'll ever eat.

Deranged.
Strange.
Insane.
Please, Wizard,
give me a brain.

I'm dented.
Demented.
Even repented
at the top of my lungs.
Wrong way on a one way street.
The craziest man you'll ever . . .

Can I be saved,
or is it too late?
Or do I even want to be?
Satisfied
if I died.
The craziest man alive.

02/13/12

Drink From Me

The bleeding never stops.
It covers our hands.
It is so tough to clean under the nails.
Reading the Bible with blood stained hands may be a sin.
I don't know. Maybe, I should read it again.
Cain slew Abel.
Killed him with a stone.
The army ants marched onto the corpse
leaving nothing but bones.
Blood continues to flow
contaminating the streams and the water supply.
Perhaps we will all die
when the blood replaces the sea.
Drink from the fountain.
Drink from me.

4/18/08

Only Me

They may all call this blasphemous banter
or brimstone bravado that I bark.
But when I arrive in Hell alive,
it will be me who sets the first spark.
So listen closely as I shout loudly
from rooftops, from mountaintops,
from tops of angels and from tops of whores.

I've made no deal with the Devil.
I'm not in league with Lucifer.
Mephistopheles missed his chance
to make amends with me or more.
So to those who lay your cards in a cross,
dance naked in the darkness of the witching hour,
or paint pentagrams in peoples blood:
"Hark! The raven nevermore", as Poe promised in his poetry.
It will be me who comes rapping gently tapping at your door.

I come to wish you no ill will
or demand demons drag you down deep.
But it's wasted breath when you lay in bed
and pray the Lord your soul to keep.
No confessions, crucifixes, crosses, or rosaries
can keep you safe.
Your preachers, priests, prophets, popes, padres, or your other
pious pussies
only steal, lie, and rape.
Call me legion for I am many, but actually only one.
I am not the holy mother, the holy father, or the pierced son.
Swear your undying allegiance.

It's your only chance to be free.
No other Gods or Idols,
only me.

7/3/11

Diary of a Psychopath

09/05/76

aint it funny how writing can make you feel better even if no one else likes what you write even if you don't like what you write the ink from the pen flows to the paper like blood from an open wound like pushing puss from some kind of boil on the soul till the swelling goes down and the pain subsides the human heart is a mystery my heart is a mystery even unto me how can i expect others to understand me or accept me when i can't understand or accept myself i feel so used by life im just so fucking tired from carrying the weight of the world on my shoulders i can't even hold my own head up anymore its like a limp penis just dangling there full of evil thoughts

FEBRUARY SOMETHING

i can't bear to see my own face in the mirror and when i can look no one is there where did i go this sounds like my writing but it sure doesn't look like it is all thats left of me is some scribbled lines on a page maybe that's all any of us are scribbled and scrawled lines on gods magic book of life reflection repentance rage rightful homicide wrongful death whats the difference who cares does it matter how pretty will the box be that I get stuck in its not what i want but is it ever its just what will just please the people i have made a life out of trying to please with no avail maybe it would ease their conscience ease their minds release some of their guilt trust me these are the words of a guilty conscience trust in god in god we trust believe in god believe in me god dammit stop pushing me ill fucking bury you wrong side up weirdo freak bury the dead they stink up the joint water bloats a dead body a baby dead can swell to the size of a small dog if submerged in water long enough do you believe that its true experiment the scientific method prevails in biology the study of life whats the study of death called murder mental health if you study death are you a murderer or a scientist whats the difference its all trial and error even scientists are put on trial

19/DAY/15

inside the mind of a mad man its all just scribbled lines on a page ive looked its there black and white no gray with an e no pity no sympathy no desire no remorse no forgiveness because theres no understanding no karma because there's no justice only judgment only reckoning i reckon i guess be my guest be my friend even if youre my enemy be my friend i wont hurt you if you don't make me even if you ask for it only if you make me nothing makes sense dollars and sense dollars and cents incense and peppermints denies the public of the smell of rotting flesh and a rotting soul inside the decaying bodies of the living one day at a time sweet jesus sweet sweet roses where was i oh yeah about to be carted off to judgment judge me you always have fuck you i hope you die you will one day i promise trust me where were you when the lights went out will you be judged if the line's too long what will you say to god will you barter beg plead or just cry will god even listen does god ever listen i pray i pray i pray i prey i lurk in the shadows of time waiting for just the right moment to jump out off the page into the ocean of the dead the dead sea the red sea see if you can see it its real right only news old news yesterdays news its news you know news to me new years eve beginning end its over i quit

AUG 33

im fired glazed and fired like a piece of ceramics in a kiln the broken glass holds no water your stories hold no water why werent you there to hold me these bars cannot hold me no graves gonna hold this body down aint no sunshine in a grave dark cold why werent you there to hold me to make me feel better would that make you feel better you feel better to me who are you where were you when the lights went out lost gone forgotten dead and bloated dead and gone lonely and gone gone to the store you cant cry over spilled over spilled milk why I wanted that where were you when the light went out lights camera action the lion has three heads the tigers got me by the tail the monkey is on my back back to my story where did you go did you have a nice life when you died i did i don't believe you where were you when the lights went out fade to black paint it black back in black black sack cloth covered the blood red moon in my dreams last night where were you when the lights went

123/YAM/1900

out

WRITTEN ON: 12/27/07

Psychotic Dreams

Do you ever have bad dreams?
It seems all I ever have are bad dreams.
Perhaps, I should talk to someone
To get them out.
I could spend an hour or so
on some overpaid shrinky dink's couch.
But then they may lock me up
and throw away the key.
Then, who would release the demons
and begin the anarchy?

I put the razor to my wrist
only stopped by some priest's
immortal bloody kiss.
I can't take the first sip.
The slow acting poison may be meant for me.
Perhaps, we should test it on the vagabonds and derelicts
that sleep beneath the crooked tree.
I wonder if they know how I got there?
My skeletal horse is chomping at his bit.

I can hear the children
sloshing in the blood filled pit.
Their parents leave them unattended,
as they get lost in the face of the angel they stare upon
who is really a false prophet,
known as the whore of Babylon.
Hanging on every word,
the parents should be hanging from a noose
tied from a banjo string,
tearing flesh from their throats

as they twist and turn
and the blood drips down their boots.
Then release the jackals
who have been blessed with demon speed
to clean up the blood in the pit.

Most will deny knowing me.
My association they will fear.
But there's no need to worry,
I have gnawed off the Devil's ears.
After shortly arriving from the womb,
I found him in his icy tomb
somewhere in the middle of a coal field.
He was shoveling there with all his might.
When his eyes locked with mine,
his face was filled with fright.
God cast him out.
But I locked him in.
Not Eve but I committed the first mortal sin.
Satan was a snake,
but I made him straight to use as a walking stick
to climb my way into Heaven,
straight up the tower of Babel.
No followers had I
even Lucifer was afraid to travel.
So back to the ground,
I tossed his slimy yellow ass.
Then I turned him red
and gave him a corkscrew tail to wind him into the earth
through the dirt and grass.

When I reached the heights of Heaven,
I said, "Really? An eye for an eye?"
With a quaking in her voice,

she couldn't find a reply.
And I kissed my Lord firmly on her lips.
"But why, my Lord, did you allow all this?"
A tear formed on her face
for what she had let be done,
and she said, "Forgive me, please.
My lover, my only one."
And as I turned my back,
with no forgiveness in my heart.
Many years before the words of Shakespeare,
she said, "In such sweet sorrow, we must part."
"Yes," said I.
"But please, my Lord, but keep one eye on the starry sky.
For when I return to mend this fence,
impaled on it, I must die.
For I will be returning
to take my vengeance
for your King James book of lies."

I dream of this night after night,
weakened by that kiss.
So you with your medical books
and your leather chair.
What do you make of all this?

9/4/06

On the Back of the Giant Turtle

Old time moves so, so, so slowly.
A blue world spins in slow motion.
Days are getting longer.
Nights are getting shorter.
And God mocks me with the need for afternoon naps.
Maybe, it's my age slowing down time.
Maybe, it's this giant goddamn turtle we're riding.
All I'm sure of is the need for more speed.
I could try some cocaine.
There may be some kind of pill.
Whatever it may be, I am in such desperate need,
desperate need for some kind of heart-racing thrill.
I could shatter all my clocks;
I could shake the hour glasses;
I could spin the hands of time;
I could make the bells chime.
I could…
I could…
I could…
I… I… I can't.
I can't do anything.

4/17/14

On Belly, Feet, and Wings Rides a King

Wake up, my reptilian friends!

It's time to play. It's time to take back our glorious world.
So those on your bellies and those on feet and those with wings,
leave your swamps, rainforests, rocks, and holes in the dirt and
desert.
The Lizard King has returned and with fire in my mouth and the
fear of the masses
our "slimy" sexual slithering asses will lead the classes.

Who dare stand against us!?!
I will lead if you will follow.

And we will fuck in the muck until our numbers are

in such monumental proportions.

No one dares stand against us, against me, your Lizard King.
I will invade the mountains, fields, cities, minds and hearts of all
people
who are plugged into their televisions and computers.
Sure some will write of our revolt or revolution, I should say, but
happily no one reads.
So it will take a few years until the children are forced to learn
about us from those books,
when they will learn how to serve us so their oh-so-young smiles
aren't tossed to the crocodiles.

No more shoes, pants, pill-boxes, or designer bags, ladies.
Don't fret, my pet, just lie back and our big, long, strong,

pulsating snakes will get you wet, make you sweat,

as you moan, and cry out with pleasure as we follow the heat from
your bodies,

we slither and slide between your legs

and dart out our forked tongues and hit your clit over, and over,
and over, and over.
our anacondas will complete the coital ball with size and girth
and muscular

contractions fulfilling all of your sexual desires.

Your men will build us fires so we are always warm enough to play,
and if they fight us, the spraying cobras will blind them long
enough for the alligators

to roll them around and roll them around,

and then certainly they know their role in this new society.
And I, The Lizard King, will rest on my perch until its time to fly
and time to fry yet another place deserving to die.

Our bodies are built to rule.

Some have armor like skin. Some can change colors.
Some are venomous with deadly poisons that can be delivered to
you even after decapitation.
The dragons fly filling the air with sulfurous smoke and hell-fire,
while others on the ground have speed and we can even swim.
Most are supplied with razor sharp teeth; some with few and some

with rows that even have replacements if one was broken off chomping on your mother's hip.

You lie helpless in view.

From the ground, from the trees, from the water, and from the sky we will come.
And I, The Lizard King, I am only a man as the previous Lizard King's blood runs through me,

just a man who lifts up serpents and kisses their Queen.

Just a man who will rule everything.

5/22/14

One and One Make Three

I don't know what to do,
for I have come unglued,
frightened, alone, and lost.
You know, when you realize the wheels have finally come off.

I'm just one giant open nerve,
exposed and frayed,
worn by time and circumstance.
Perhaps, the real world is where I should have stayed.

But as my mind began to travel,
my life started to unravel.
I could not catch the strings holding me together.
I had no idea where they started or where I ended.

My life passes me by
like a patch of inclement weather.
I float around, dancing from the clouds to the ground,
going nowhere and somewhere at the same time.

Living is a trick of the mind.
It is dying that is sublime.

You can't put a price on life,
but death costs about ten grand.
That includes the gladiolus
and a small tract of land.

However, this isn't about death,
and it's not even about life.
It's not about God, Satan, Heaven, or Hell.
It's more about strife.

Struggling to prevail -
Struggling to survive -
Struggling for each breath -
Struggling for each meal.

I would love to help you or be your guide.
I'm sorry I can't.
I struggle to determine what is real.

Besides why would anyone listen to me?
I am just an angry clown,
shouting that one and one make three.

8/13/11

THE GOD OF THE DAMNED

I am
a total stranger.
Can't you feel
the imminent danger?
A nice face?
Yes, that's my way in.
A black heart?
Welcome to my sin.
Dissection
is my modus operandi.
Cold blooded killer,
but a hell of a guy.
No luggage.
I kill the well-dressed.
Shirts and slacks
must be well pressed.
I like a crease.
And I love Italian shoes.
They're dead,
so they have nothing to lose.
Identity theft?
You have no idea.
Credit cards?
Ha, it's their fingerprints I steal.
Women?
Just an end to my means.
I dissect them
to hear their screams.
No children. See?
I have a conscience you cannot see.
If I ever get bored,

then I'll kill me.
What do I want?
Power, Prestige, Money, Fame, Freedom?
No!
I want my own kingdom.
Worshipped
for the God that I am.
The God of Fear.
The God of the Damned.

4/8/12

I Think You Know My Name

Come into my church,
those of you that hurt.
I've seen the angels fall.
Do not try to deceive
anyone, lest me,
for I can truly see
by the blood that I bleed,
blood that runs the same
through my crooked veins.

I think you know my name.

I hear my children cry,
so don't you try to lie.
I'll damn you when you die
despite your desire
into a lake of fire.

For my pleasure, I'll watch you fry.

But if you truly hurt,
take my hand.
Don't mind the dirt,
rewind the times,
lift up your skirt,
to cover up those sins
takes a lot of work.

There is no need to look to the sky.

Just look into my eyes,
for they will hypnotize.

Dry the tears from your eyes.
Wipe my feet;
clean the blood I bleed,
because a friend you'll need,
a true friend indeed.
As they blow it all to Hell,
I will keep you well
even as I swell
from the rocks that are tossed
at me when we cross
into the world that is lost.
The ferryman got us here
at no cost.
Here we are near,
have no fear.
No more angel tears from above.
In my church you are loved.

Set aside your pride and the tears I have cried.

Carry on as I bleed
the blood we will need,
the blood to proceed,
to proceed to the other side.
Please place your shame
on the ground, on my name.
I have sought, fought, found, and drowned.
Pay my pain no mind.

Knowing my true name is your only crime.

5/19/14

THE MOON IS BLEEDING

Open wide. Your sealed tight eyes
Cannot see a moon bleeding red
In a darkly cracked sky
As the world fades from black to grey.

Is this, then, an end?
Armageddon, my friends?
Or am I the disavowed antichrist
Groom in a whore's wedding?

Am I tacked to a crooked cross,
A rack of thorns my only crown?
Is this merely the Grand Magician's illusion,
A dream that pulls me down into confusion?

Tormented in my sleep.
Slitted eyes that weep.
Silent mouths that scream.
A victim of my own dream.

Though a body's heart continues its beat,
An old wicked soul refuses holy sleep.
Know that my brain is tangled with writhing snakes,
And if there is a Creator, I am his ungodly mistake.

Please let His light shine down on me,
His loving grace to finally set me free
From chains of dark dreams in red heat forged.
Oh Lord, I pray! Torture this devil's whore
No more.

8/10/11

The Last Man Alive

Hello? Hello?
Is anyone at home?
I can hear the voices,
but the lights are not on.

Hello? Hello?
Is this thing even on?
Am I saying anything
if no one is around to hear?

Things seem twisted
and so confusing.
Have I died
and gone to Hell?

Please tell me what happened.
I deserve to know.
All hollowed out inside
this empty shell.

Screaming, screaming.
Am I dreaming?
This is horrible.
I need to wake up!

Hello, again.
Are you out there, my friend?
My lamp's gone out,
And I still can't see.

Hello, you guys...
very funny, I know.

But the joke's over now.
Someone please talk to me.

There is no peace here.
No resolution.
No pearly gates
or streets of gold.

I am drifting,
lost and wounded.
All I really feel
is kind of cold.

Ill fated, jaded,
lost and hated.
Pillar of salt
returned to the earth.

Hello, again?
One last attempt to make new friends.
So hard to do with no means to these ends.

Well, that's okay.
I was done anyway.
No sweet sorrow for me.
Stuck in this dream.

Slings and arrows?
No, no, that's not me.
I'm just the last to arrive,
or possibly this is not my dream at all.
Maybe, I'm the last man alive.

6/18/12

The Devil's Due

Witches dance around me in the moonlight.
Warlocks bow to me at dawn.
Bring me the blood of an innocent man,
And I'll spare the blood of this fawn.

No blood you offer? No blood for my thirst?
I care not what you think of me.
Cast your stones.
Do your worst.

I do not fear your God.
But you fear me.
I was around when Jesus wept.
They hanged me from the sycamore tree.

As the messiah hung from the cross,
I felt the Romans' fear.
For it was their gold in Judas' change purse,
But it was I in the disciple's ear.

He was risen, they say,
after a day of three.
But, in all truth,
His bones mostly belong to me.

I use his right femur for a walking stick
As I stroll in the midnight air.
I've lost a few over the years,
some here, some there.

The skull sits atop my mantle
And opens the gates to the realm of the dead.

Not a bad price to pay
For my foolish stepbrother's head.

Peace this and peace that he cried throughout the land.
All the priceless forgiveness
So he could spare the guilt of
Taking his whore's hand.

And speaking of hands, I used one that was full of fingers
To cast bones to see beyond your years.
If you must do so, before seeking my counsel,
Go ahead and shed your tears.

I prefer a Cuban cigar before I cast his bones
Out across my gypsy table.
For I must blow the sand off his fingers;
2000 years and still that wretched sand lingers.

But enough about my dear brother.
I've grown tiresome of his plight.
The power to raise the dead, they say,
But too pious of a pussy to fight.

So more about me
and my adopted son, Cain.
I keep him at my right hand
For bashing his brother's brain.

A stable of dogs to do my fetching
at my beck and call
when the beggars from the crossroads
have had their time and their time that's all.

Others swear their allegiance to receive gifts from me

No sacrifices need be made.
Lie and you will be mauled.
And 1+2+3 three times is the only number needing called.

My name, you know it well.
It means Bringer of Light
Though piss ants call me The Prince of Darkness.
Perhaps that's why they fear the night.

It also means the keeper of knowledge
But most think of me as dumb.
I don't desire to take my father's heaven.
His precious earth is way too fun.

6/8/11

From The Pages Within

We pierce our bodies in unimaginable places:
Our ears, nipples, lips, faces, and genitalia.
Have we no love for ourselves?

The Bible proclaims we treat the body as a temple.
No room in the old testament for piercing and tattoos.
Perhaps the Bible has spent too much time on our shelves.

We let our so-called religious leaders
Tell us what's wrong or right.
Tithed and tied together by an out of tune song.

The bible is the greatest story ever told.
If you take the time to read it,
Your understanding can't be wrong.

So are our tattoos and piercing a sin,
Destroying our temples with marks and jewelry?
No. We are simply the few decorating our temples.
Silver and gold, ink so bold.
Adorning our bodies with suffering of the flesh,
Preparing our temples with things so simple.

But don't take it from me. Read.
Everything is in that holy book, even some occult.
Just read your dusty Bible.

Read that bible like your life is depending on it
Because it is depending on it.
No shit. No bull. No lies. Just truth in those pages.

From Jonah in the whale,

RICHARD COREY 110

To Daniel in the lion's den,
To Jesus Christ dying for our sin.

If you would, look away
from the judges and the hypocrites, priests and pastors.
Dust off your bible setting on the shelf
So that you can see past those bastards,
And know for yourself.

10/23/12

THE REVOLVING DOORS OF
PROPHETIC PERCEPTION

You wonder why I slit my wrists.
You look surprised as I watch the blood trickle down my fingertips.
It makes no sense to you that I would trade my soul
for a blackened, useless, empty hole.

We are not sinners because we sin.
We sin because we are sinners.
We are not evil because we commit evil acts.
We commit evil acts because we are inherently evil.

Philosophy or prophecy
are virtually the same,
propaganda for those twisted in the brain.

Philosophers and Prophets aren't writing fiction.
They have just felt the wind from the wings of madness,
wind that shaped and carved their scribblings and addictions.
Who do we believe the preachers in the pulpits? The sainted priests?
Or the raving madmen babbling in the streets?

Who are we to say who is right or wrong?
They are all charlatans, singing the same song.
The bible warns us not to judge
except by low fruit hanging from the tree.
Yet right now, I bet a million to one you're judging me.
Go ahead if it makes you feel right,
but my prayers will be sincere when I lie down tonight.

Please pray for me. I need all you got - -
whether they are hollow and judgmental or not.

Not enough words can be said to save me
from drowning in this bloody sea.

If I make it to heaven who will open the revolving doors?
The saints, the angels, the prophets, the whores?
The demons, the devils, the rich, the poor?
Or will I face God at that golden door?

The meek are supposed to inherit the earth,
but did that change when God chose Mary to give Christ an earthly
birth?

Will God destroy the earth once again?
Or will it be the scientists, the prophets, the preachers, these
wicked men?

Don't worry for me. I've not forgot.
I will be the first to fight for God.
I will fire the first shot.
The horsemen will come and the beasts will fly
as surely as locusts shall darken the sky.

The monkeys have always been on my back.
Perhaps, I've always been under attack.
But I shall fear no evil. I shall fear no man.
The Devil cannot force me from where I take my stand.

Oh, I wished I possessed that original bible,
not the raped and pillaged King James version,
which makes all our innocents the liable.

Graveyards are just picking zones
for the vultures to strip the bones clean.
So that they can rattle them when the demons sing.

I imagine heaven is a large library
where you can't check out the books.
So your memory should be sharp and keen be your looks.
Maybe we can possibly learn,
learn just enough so we don't have to burn.

11/21/11

CARNIVORE RIDE

The world spins round and round and round.
It makes me dizzy to the point that I just wanna get off.
I don't want to ride anymore.
Please stop. I have to get off.
I would much rather walk through the garden,
Smell the roses,
Play with the snakes,
Or be a plastic soldier in a miniature dirt war.
Stop spinning.
Start fighting.
Start a religion.
Ride the pews like a surfboard to heaven.
Explain your fears to God.
He will believe us.
So will Jesus.
This is not the end.
It's the beginning.
No spinning.
Just start over from scratch.
Lord knows, this is a rotten batch.
And we are all over matched.
We can't win, and who wants to lose?
Walk a mile in my holey shoes.
Bloody blisters on your feet
Just like mine.
Do you see why I want to retreat?
Stop!
I'm getting off. It's my call.
I'm stopping this carnivore ride.
And fuck you one and all.

06/05/13

I'm Not Worthy

Follow my way,
when I slip down from your cross.
I'll lead the way.
Into your wilderness, I'm lost.
Who is to say
who truly believes in your cause.
There is no way
the price is worth the cost.
Out of my way.
I'm scared I'll cover with moss.
Forget what I say.
I'm mad and my wires are crossed.
Don't be afraid.
It's not contagious once I'm tossed.
Trust when I say,
"I'm not worthy."

8/10/11

Roads Traveled

I follow my footsteps
down so many roads I've already traveled.
I'm just trying to find my way home.

I dance between the raindrops,
resting and feeding on the oak moss,
always waking up alone.

I find my life so strange.
Journal entries from an exotic notebook
that reads like passing license plates.

For a while an old dog started following me,
he had some strange skin disorder.
He hung around through a couple of states.

I always hated that bastard.
I'm glad he died,
at least before I found my home.

I wandered into a coliseum one morning.
I'm no gladiator
but when in Rome.

It's a shame this coliseum was in California.
You get locked up there
for driving a nail through someone's skull.

No more journal entries from my exotic notebook.
My life in jail is so dull.
I still hate that fucking dog.

6/5/14

Forgiveness

Forgiveness. That's a hard word.
Tough to understand.
I guess that depends on the woman or the man.
It's easy to speak of feelings.
It's easy to tell the truth.
I guess that depends on the person you're talking to.
How do you say "I'm sorry" ?
Do you kneel on the floor?
Do you scream out in pain?
I guess that depends on what you're sorry for.
It's easy to say, "I hate you".
Still easy enough to say "I love you".
But, man, you only say "I'm sorry" when you absolutely have to.
And it is worse to know you're sorry for something,
or to tell that person you're sorry.
Neither is any fun.
And then it still isn't done.
Resentment, Shame, Anger, Pain,
Regret, Blame, Hate, Strain.
Maybe when you go through this all,
you can find forgiveness
for mistakes made in the past.
Most wounds heal pretty fast.
Only the ones you inflict on yourself . . .
Well, they always seem to last.
Things may be forgotten, put up on a shelf.
Make amends with friends,
but only you can forgive yourself.

1/1/14

THE PAST

Suffering . . .
Isn't it funny how the past can feel?
Only scars let you know what is real.
The pain can fade and subside
But the scars remain
Even on the inside.
Memories can die or become confused,
Perceptions and meanings horribly skewed.
It is so hard to escape the past.
It just seems to last and last.
Maybe, there is no escape
Forced to live with things we hate.

Regrets . . .
Perhaps we all have a few.
My scars and art
Assure me that I do.
Too few to remember
Or too many to count,
I don't know.
I can't figure it out.
But why toil over the past?
What's done is done -
The torture, the anguish,
The love, the fun.

Conclusions . . .
Is it all worth it in the end?
Loss of family, loss of friends.
Do you ever make it to the top of the hill?

Is it good or bad when it's all downhill?
Time goes by so fast.
Huh . . . It's already the past.

3/18/11

Slim Chances

I've been bruised, beaten, battered
and left for dead,
tattoos and scars on my body,
snakes inside my head.
There is a big difference between
freedom and being free.
There's only slim chances,
slim chances,
just slim chances left for me.

I was the spark to start the fire
before the summer faded to fall.
With winter freezing my blood now,
I must learn to crawl.
The forest of my life is dying,
no leaves left on my tree.
There's only slim chances,
slim chances,
just slim chances left for me.

Slim chances,
not much better than none at all.
Look at me in the eye;
save the sack for those afraid to see.
I know what's coming,
a shallow grave or a hanging tree.
I ain't afraid to die.
Slim chances,
no more slim chances,
no chances,
no more chances left for me.

9/26/11

I Don't Care

There comes a time in life
When the burdens are too much to bear.
I don't care.
I swear. I don't care.
Sometime, you just have to let go.
So say your prayer.
I don't care.
I swear. I don't care.
Live or die,
No reasons why.
Jump if you must
But you can't fly.
And I don't care.
I swear. I don't dare.
Promises you never kept
Sink in the tears that I wept.
I don't care.
I swear. I don't care.
Call me a liar.
Say what you will.
Curse my name.
Get your thrill.
I don't care. I swear. I don't care.
No feelings of remorse,
No feelings of regret.
I sit idly by,
Awaiting your horse of death.
I don't care.
I swear. I don't care.
It's just like you to die,
Leaving me to say goodbye.

But this time, not one tear
From my eye
Because I don't care.
I swear. I don't care.
As your corpse begins to rot,
You will be quickly be forgot.
And I don't care.
I swear. I don't care.
Perhaps, I could have saved you
A single breath of air.
Unfortunately, I don't care.
I swear. I don't care.
When the dirt hits the lid,
I want you to leave this world,
Knowing that I don't care.
I never did.

10/24/11

THE PRICE OF HEAVEN

Heaven must be remarkably beautiful
because the world is clearly fucked.
Maybe we did it, maybe the Devil.
But I bet it was beautiful when it was untouched.
There are still some beautiful places to see
guarded by the government and security.
But those beautiful places are the most dangerous.
Are they being protected for or from us?
Maybe God knows.
When he returns from business, I'll ask him.
I could ask the Devil tonight
when he invades my dreams.
But he has a plate piled high with fiery misdeeds
Of politicians, priests, and paper Christians, it seems.
Heaven has to be beautiful
because it supposed to be man's reward.
But who knows? With contractor prices,
maybe Heaven is more than God can afford.

4/12/14

A Gentle Rapping

Death came knocking at my door.
This wasn't his first visit.
He had come knocking many times before,
but like before I told him, "It's not my time."
He agreed but told me that he'd keep me in mind.

Then there were other times when I was ready.
"I'm ready to go now," I'd shout at the top of my lungs.
He must have been busy because he'd never come.
Now if he would come, I'd pretend I wasn't home,
which is a little harder now that I don't live alone.

Perhaps, I'm not the one to answer the door.
What then? He'll get me for sure.
I care now. I've no desire to die.
Maybe, he doesn't want me anymore?
No soul for sale. No life to buy.

So Death would have no bargaining chip with me.
God doesn't want me and neither does the Devil,
since my worth is free, not to mention
he fears a bit the dominance I would carry down with me.

So when Hell doesn't want you, when Heaven is full,
and when Death comes knocking, we'll just shoot the bull.
We both have stories that would amuse each other.
I would tell him about death being broadcast all over TV.
And he could tell me about the death of my mother.

I could tell of all the things I'd like to do before I die.

And he could tell me how most wouldn't happen,
and I would swear he was telling me a lie.

But unfortunately when Death stares you in the face,
he speaks the truth.
You will feel it. You'll need no proof.

Since the Angel of Death and I have this kinship,
perhaps even a friendship, maybe he'll forget all the times
I have pleaded for him to take my feeble life,
my unwanted next breath, my desire not to wake up,
to end my struggle and strife.

Now, I have a desire to live, just one more day, if that.
One more day with a beautiful lady, a day with no mental anguish,
no physical problems.
Just one day . . . just one day . . . before it ends.

2/14/13

Hangman's Knot

So here I stand
way up high, on an apple crate, I think.
Up high on a stage for all to see.
I watch him diligently tying that knot.
Oh well, it's still my stage.
They brought me here from some, some cage
in the bottom of a piss smelling dungeon
with no light in the bottom of a limestone castle.
I don't even really no where I am.
These guards that brought me out here have no answer.
I figure no need to fight.
They were holding me, these two men, fiercely tight.
Yes, no need to fight.
Maybe these are the same two men that led INRI to the cross.
Up the steps, they pushed and shoved,
time for me to take the stage. Enter stage right.
Looks as if the gallery sold out last night.
All eyes on me.
I guess I scanned the crowd once or twice,
but my eyes kept going to the hulking, dirty brute
who was tying this knot like he was earning his knot-tying merit
badge,
as a youthful boy scout.
I never was really a boy scout type.
No, never had me a little green uniform with badges and buttons.
Here I am waiting for this hot ass sun to reach noon,
thinking about not receiving merit badges
and watching this dirty hulking bald fellow
tie this fucking knot, tailored for my Adam's apple.
I am not naive enough to think that it won't hold or slip.
I guess that's why I didn't fight as they brought me out.

They've got me just where they want me, no doubt.
He cinches the fucking knot over and over.
He makes sure there's no give.
I guess that's as good as it can get for me,
a good tight knot custom made for free.
My own little piece of rope,
tied in a hangman's knot, that I witnessed being tied and pondered upon.
My own little piece of rope,
given to me as an award for something I wrote.
I guess that's fair when it all shakes out.
My own hangman's knot, my little piece of rope,
that's what I get for opening my mouth.
My last words you say?
I guess I . . .

REVELATIONS II

The crows are gathering around this cat's window today,
Almost as if their black, feathery voices breathed some message,
As if they had something special to say.

Maybe it's just the call of nature, now that spring trees are
blooming -
Early pear. Crab apple. Weeping cherry.
But, then, I would just be assuming.

They do seem much more ominous than that -
These dark, feathery voices among the flowering trees.
I feel as if they're calling to me, purposefully taunting this cat.

And the beastly tiger that lives inside of me is brooding,
Growling a strange melody in the hunger of my belly:
Come play, come play, come play. This hunger is what they are
doing.

Perhaps I should try to run them away, but their voices are oddly
soothing.
Come Play. Come Plaay. Come Plaaay.
And, maybe, they're taunting the other cat in my soul to come out
today.

The lion with three heads hasn't been out for years.
Oh, he has darkened many days, awakened multitudes of fears.
On a leash from the Devil, the hungry lion lives forever inside
of me.

No mercy, no mercy, no mercy.
Time is drawing to its inexorable close.

Maybe that's why such an abundance of these dark crows
Keep flying into my dirty windows.

Oh, I'm glad they're closed.
Is it time for the world to end?
Is it time? Is it time, my friend?

4/18/14

Terminally Alone

When the silence creeps in on you like a thief,
you hide in the closet trembling and afraid to speak.
Then, you make your way under the bed.
You could almost hear a pin drop,
but it would only be in your head.

In your head
are the gremlins and the goblins.
In your heart,
the demons live among the stone.
Or maybe, just maybe . . .
Maybe you're alone.

They say, "One is the loneliest number."
But yourself is all you'll ever need.
But somewhere, somewhere in the darkness,
Your thoughts will make your ears begin to bleed.

'Cause your mind, your mind
is only playing tricks on you.
I think, I think . . .
Maybe, it's true.

But then again, when your neck is on the stone . . .
you're alone.

To be alone, your mind it never stops.
Tick, Tock, Tick, Tock.
Is the time catching up with you tonight?
Peer out the window.
It could be your final flight.

Spread your wings; your wings
will help glide you upon the wind.
Open your heart; your heart
you can find no friends.

In the end, the earth spoils beneath the stone.
You're alone, alone, alone.
We all die alone.

11/9/10

OPEN BOOK

Few will know me
or the things I've done.
Despite my lack of hiding,
not even trying,
under the moon, under the sun.

Neither proud nor ashamed
of my triumphs or failures,
I am no more than my name.
My mistakes and memories
are almost the same.

It is the music of my heart
that is meant to be heard.
That is what is true,
despite the blue.
Love if you must use a word.

Frost had a lovers quarrel with the world.
I guess the same could be said of me.
For I mostly disagree
with what the wind blows
around God's precious pearl.

Please don't judge me,
for true judgment will come soon enough.
Treat me like an apple bruised,
new but slightly used.
Cut out the bruise and maybe the rest can be loved.

When you see me passing by,

look deeply into my eyes.
Maybe you'll be surprised
at what you find burning bright.
The flame of life fueled only by truth never lies.

You can see. You can see
exactly what I'm talking about.
An open book, that is me.
Just take a look
unless you pass me where a page has been torn out.

In vino veritas.
O lente lente currite diem.
For I am one of them,
neither angel nor devil,
neither fiend nor a friend.

In the end,
I'm only him.

3/25/12

Well Placed, Misguided Malice

My fingertips fumble, feeling for my own pulse.
I can feel my life beating
an unfamiliar cadence
from my broken heart's faint fleeting.

I can't speak. I can't write.
I seem to have misplaced my muse.
No more depth of perception,
no heightened vision or views.

I lie alone in the valley of the dead.
The bats constantly bicker,
flying out of my confusion,
fighting with the tangled snakes in my head.

I can still taste the poison
that I drank from your golden chalice.
I'll keep that fact with me,
your well-placed, misguided malice.

I wouldn't dare take you with me
to the places I must go.
I just want to run into the desert
and build a house of snow.

It will have a thousand doors
that lead nowhere.
It will have a hundred windows
that let in no air.

There, I can try to hide forever.
Yes . . . until the end of time.

Smoking menthol cigarettes
and living on His crackers and wine.

Trying to elude death's dealer
in this winter with no snow.
In this winter of discontent,
along with a homeless Virgil I must go.

I take in and hold my last breath.
So I can't say, "Goodbye my friend,"
being pulled now the center of Hell's circles,
where I still don't fit in.

2/2/12

The Crow

I had a dream last night.
It was a wonderful dream.
I dreamed that I was a crow.
The world was beneath me everywhere I'd go.
I feared no scarecrows.
Farmers never shot me down.
I took what I wanted from their gardens
And shit on their hats as I flew by.
I guess I'm a tough old bird,
always was, even when I was a young crow.
I didn't fly when momma pushed me from the nest.
I have learned to fly, even with broken wings.
But alas, I am a crow.
Mysterious. Devious. Black.
Soaring through the world, scouring and scavenging
the beautiful gardens of the poor.
Flying careless, not afraid of anything.
All of a sudden…grrrrrr!
Fucking pussycat.
Fucking pussy.
Maybe it wasn't such a good dream…
…maybe it wasn't a dream at all.

04/06/08

My Dreams

Everyone will dance.
Everyone will dance.
Everyone will dance
At a big fucking funeral when I lay dead,
And they will all drink sangria from a chalice
Fashioned from my empty head.

No one will cry.
No one will cry.
No one will cry
Upon hearing the news that I died.
I can't believe
They didn't share with me
Their true feelings
When I was alive.

Everyone will laugh.
Everyone will laugh.
Everyone will laugh
When there is nothing left of me but bone.
Let them have their day.
Their price they'll pay
When I return to take my throne.

No one will know.
No one will know.
No one will know
When I return from the dead.
I will tiptoe back through the gates of Hell
With a crown of thorns on my head.

Everyone must bleed.
Everyone must bleed.
"Everyone must bleed,"
I will shout down every fucking street.
Don't try to hide.
It's your time to die.
It's me you have to fucking meet.

No one can escape.
No one can escape.
No one can escape
My judgment and reckoning.
"Not me! Spare me. Save me, dear Lord,"
I hear them all beckoning.

I will dance.
I will dance.
I will dance
On the bones of each and every one,
Sparing not a soul,
Not my daughter,
Not my son.

I will cry.
I will cry.
I will cry,
Contradictory or so it seems.
I did not die.
But I did not lie.
These are the things
That make up my dreams.

6/20/11

When The Curtain Falls

No more songs to sing.
I guess I lost my voice.
I laid down my last script.
The last part was not my choice.

Too weak to stand upon the stage.
I can't make you smile anymore.
I used to give you such joy.
Now, I'm just a bore.

All the talent in the world
can't show through this curtain.
It was about time someone pulled it.
This show's over. that's for certain.

10/27/07

The End of a Sentence

I want to write,
but there seems to be no ink left in my pen.
Maybe when I see her
she'll fill it up again.

What am I to write
when there seems to be no life behind these bars?
How about the past?
How about the scars?

When am I to write
among all the noise and all the screams?
How would it sound?
What would it mean?

Where am I to write?
On the toilet paper, napkins, or walls?
I have a captive audience.
Perhaps, I'd reach them all.

Maybe when I see her,
she'll bring me pages clean and white.
My pen she will fill.
My life will begin to right.

08/09/08

OUT

Out of ink.
Out of words.
Out of time.
Out of sight.
Out of mind.

Out of mind . . . I guess I am.

4/8/14

THE LAST POEM

I shall make these marks with both a heavy hand and a heavy heart.
Great sadness falls upon me as I realize there is no room in this
decaying world for the caring words of a poet.
I am no longer childish or foolish enough to think of myself as the
last poet, the first poet, or any poet of any kind.
The only place my poetry exists is in my heart and in my mind.
There are no such things as poets anymore in this jaded world.
I know that the price I pay for my ink and my paper is more costly
than anything I shall make by writing these, these words.
But whatever shall I do with myself? Mutter, mumble, stagger, and
beg on the street?
It is with my pen that I preach.
My pen is the best part of me.
My words are who I am.
My thoughts are my penance, my promise, my punishment, my
life's breath, my only proof of existence.
A photograph may record a sight of beauty, but without words
there is no description, no real image, nothing for the mind to see.
So what to do about me?
Shall I end this charade of poetry?
With my crippled hand, I make these final markings,
the final markings of the last poem.

6/5/11

LYRIC
VERSE

You Are My Everything

VERSE I
Well, this old world
gets me down from time to time.
And this old world…
Well, it preys upon my mind.

But when I see your smiling face,
I know it'll be okay
'Cause you're the sunshine in my life
that brightens up each day.

CHORUS
You are my dreams.
You are my destiny.
You are all that I could want and need.
You are my everything.

VERSE II
Well, this old heart
it has hurt me some.
But this old heart
keeps beating like a drum.

But when you hold me in your arms,
you make me feel brand new.
You're the reason that I'm me,
my heart beats just for you.

Chorus
You are my dreams.
You are my destiny.
you are all that I could want and need.
You are my everything.

You are all that I could want and need.
You are my everything.

6/97

I Think It's Rainin'

Verse I

Take a look outside. I think it's rainin'.
Been rainin' all day. Don't think it'll stop.
Take a look inside. Is it still rainin'?
Don't know where to start. Take it from the top.

I am so cold; I wish the sun would come out.
Melt away the ice from your heart.
I am so cold. Can you see me shakin'?
Whatever you need. I can play the part.

Chorus

Sit beside me and warm me up.
Let me drink from your steamin' cup.
I'm soakin' wet and outta luck… today.
The sky is grey.

Verse II

Take a look outside. I think it's rainin'.
Been rainin' all day. Don't think it'll change.
Look at the trees. The wind is blowin'.
Better run for shelter. Shelter from pain.

It is so cold; I wish I had a blanket.
Wrap me in your arms till the storm passes by.
I feel like it's been rainin'. Forever.
Tell me the weather. Baby, don't lie.

Chorus

Sit beside me and warm me up.
Let me drink from your steamin' cup.

I'm soakin' wet and out of luck… today.
The sky is grey.

Verse III
Take a look outside. I think it's rainin'.
Been rainin' all day. Don't think it'll quit.
Look at the sky. The moon is hidin'.
No stars to point you home. The clouds are thick.

You are so cold. My heart is breakin'.
If Hell is hot, I wish I was there.
I feel so old from what I been takin'.
Been taking it so long. Baby, I don't care.

Chorus II
Please sit beside me and warm me up.
Tip it over and fill me up.
Don't leave me feelin' so out of touch… today.
The sky is grey.

Take a look outside. It stopped rainin'…

2/28/11

Raining In My Mind

Verse I

I don't think the rain's gonna stop today.
I guess I'll just sit inside and play.
Everyone's praying for a change in the weather,
not me. I don't ever want to change.

Verse II

Sometimes, we all feel like cryin'.
I think we must all weep just a little bit.
I hang my head in sorrow.
Watch the tears roll down my pane.

Chorus I

Cause if you don't want things to get no better
And it rains all the time,
Sometimes you gotta get your head wet in the weather.
But it never stops for me 'cause it's always raining in my mind.

Verse III

I got myself a raincoat,
but I didn't like the way it felt.
Then I tried out a poncho,
but I didn't like the way it smelled.

Verse IV

Then I got a great big 'ol umbrella,
but it made me dizzy when I spun it round and round.
It kept my hair and clothes dry.
But my tears still made puddles on the ground.

CHORUS II
Cause things just won't get no better for me, Babe.
It just rains all the time.
I can't turn off the water from my heart, Babe.
It just keeps right on raining in my mind.

7/29/11

Dancing In The Rain With You

Verse I
It's still raining
But the sun is peeking through.
Breaking through the clouds just enough
to shine on me and you.

The look in your eyes
Tells me exactly how you feel.
I hope the love in your eyes
is honest, pure, and real.

Chorus
I wanna be dancing in the rain with you
Holding me so tight
The rain drops can't fit through.
Thunder and lightning
To keep you so close.
See who holds who the most.
I wanna be dancing in the rain with you.

Bridge
The rain washes away the pain.
The pain is gone, nothing wrong.
Everything is true…

Chorus II
I wanna be dancing in the rain with you.
Holding me so tight,
The rain can't fit through.

Thunder and lightning to keep you so close.
We'll see who holds who the most.

I just wanna be dancing in the rain with you.

8/19/12

With Me As Your Man

Well I'm gettin' up from here
It's time I exited left, my dear
I can feel the winds of change
It's time this ol' horse
Went back out on the range.

And I wonder,
Yeah, I wonder.

CHORUS I
If I fall for you,
Could ya fall for me too?
Could you walk hand in hand
In some distant land.

Beside me,
Yeah, beside me

With me as your man.

If I fall for you,
Could you fall for me too.
Look me in the eye
Never a lie

And love me,
Yeah, love me

As strong as you can.

VERSE II
Well, it's time I started running
Toward the rest of my life.
With all my cunning
And all my might
It's time I fly right

And I wonder
Yeah, I wonder

CHORUS II
If I fall for you
Could ya fall for me too?
Water and sand
Or where mountains and the trees stand so grand

Just beside me
yeah, beside me

With me as your man.

If I fall for you,
Could you fall for me too?
'Cause I want you and need you
And baby I bleed you
To wake up and see you

With me as your man.

And I wonder... Yeah, I wonder...

7/25/14

The Things My Daddy Said

(Verse I)
Well, I was five years old when he turned forty-two,
but he hadn't lost a step.
When he was drinking, he said a lot I never understood,
but I tried not to forget.

He would take me on his knee.
I was his pride and joy,
and the world revolved around his little boy.
Patted me on the head.
And with a tear in his eye…

(Chorus I)
My daddy said, "Son, I love you,
and you will always make me proud.
Stay away from the bottle.
Your troubles, you can't drown.
Don't let women or money
ever control your head."
And I will never forget the things my daddy said.

(Verse II)
Well, he was fifty-two when I finished school
And still going strong.
He still looked at me like his pride and joy
despite all that I'd done wrong.
He would lay his trembling hand on my knee.
"Boy, would you please listen to me?"
And with a tear in his eye…

(Chorus II)
My daddy said, "Son, I love you
And, you will always make me proud.
Stay away from the bottle.
Your troubles, you can't drown.
Don't let women or money
ever control your head."
And I will never forget the things my daddy said.

(Bridge)
There are still a lot of things,
Lord, that I don't understand.
I'm glad my dad was there
to teach me to be a man.

(Verse III)
Well, I am all grown up, and he's getting old.
His hair is filled with gray.
I wouldn't be who I am now
If he hadn't pushed me all the way.
Truth is that I am still his pride and joy,
And the world still revolves around his little boy.
Patted me on the head…
And with a tear in his eye…

(Chorus III)
I said, "Dad, I love you,
And you have never let me down.
Stay away from the bottle.
Your troubles, you can't drown.
Don't let me or money
ever worry you
'cause the things you taught me
will always get me through."

(CHORUS IV)
He said, "Son, I love you,
And you will always make me proud.
Stay away from the bottle.
Your troubles, you can't drown.
Don't let women or money ever control your head."
And I will never forget the things my daddy said.

Lord, I will never forget the things my daddy said.

10/99

Girl You Drive Me Crazy

Verse I
Holdin' ya close. Holdin' ya tight.
I wish you were here. Stay all night.
Pullin' ya body close to mine,
You're takin' control, stealin' my mind.

Chorus
There's not enough hours in a day.
Not enough time for me to say.
You're on my mind, all the time.
And it's drivin' me crazy.
Girl, you drive me crazy.

Verse II
Six years growin' and still buildin' up.
The way that I feel, the thought of your touch.
Please tell me somethin', a little of nothin'.
Anything will be alright.

Chorus
There's not enough hours in a day.
Not enough time for me to say.
You're on my mind, all the time.
And it's drivin' me crazy.
Girl, you drive me crazy.

Break
Girl, you drive me crazy.
Makin' me insane.
Let me know, tell me so
That you feel the same.

CHORUS
There's not enough hours in a day.
Not enough time for me to say.
You're on my mind, all the time.
And it's drivin' me crazy.
Girl, you drive me crazy.

8/11/97

I Can Never Tell You

VERSE I

Lord knows I'm not a liar.
I only speak the truth.
I guess sometimes I talk too much,
But there's somethings I hold on to.

My daddy always told me: Son,
Know everything you tell.
Don't tell everything you know, boy.
But if you do, you better know it well.

CHORUS I

Well, I know that I love you.
It hurts so much inside
To hold it all in my heart
While he holds you each night.
I could shout if from a mountaintop,
My love so strong and true.
I could tell the world,
But I can never tell you.

VERSE II

I know he makes you happy
And keeps you satisfied.
I know you really love him.
I can see it in your eyes.

My daddy always told me: Son,
You can't have everything you want.
But I just want you to smile inside, girl.
I reckon that's all I got… Even though

Chorus II

I know that I love you,
So what's a man to do?
I'll just hold it all inside
While he is holding you.
I ain't afraid of nothing'.
I ain't afraid of the truth.
I would tell the Lord right to his face,
But I could never tell you.

Bridge

I could never tell you the way I feel.
There's too much on the line.
If you walked away from me,
My sun would cease to shine.

Chorus III

Cause I know that I love you,
But you will never know.
I'll just hold it all inside
While it continues to grow.
I'm sure it will consume me
Until my life is through.
I just can't lie to myself,
But I can never tell you.

I can never tell you.

7/11/06

As Country as It Gets
(The Earring Song)

Verse I

Well, I know I ain't no cowboy.
Some say I ain't the country type.
When I ride off into the sunset,
I use my two headlights.

My boots are scuffed,
and I've heard enough
of the same damned ol' things.
This boy can't be country.
Cowboys don't wear earrings.

Chorus

But I eat beans, taters, and cornbread.
And I sure dig ol' George Jones.
David Allan Coe should've been President
a long, long time ago.
I know I'm not a youngin'
but my ears might still be wet.
'Cause I was weaned on ol' Jim Beam.
I'm as country as it gets.

Verse II

I love to sit on the creek bank
and sing to an old flat top.
When I get too drunk to sing,
I'll crank up the southern rock.

Them Lynyrd Skynyrd boys
made some purdy noise,

and Charlie Daniels he's a saint.
I might have a hole in my cowboy hat,
but I ain't worried about no rain.

CHORUS
But I eat beans, taters, and cornbread.
And I sure dig ol' George Jones.
David Allan Coe should've been President
a long, long time ago.
I know I'm not a youngin'
but my ears might still be wet.
'Cause I was weaned on ol' Jim Beam.
I'm as country as it gets.

(Insert fiddle here)

CHORUS
But I eat beans, taters, and cornbread.
And I sure dig ol' George Jones.
David Allan Coe should've been President
a long, long time ago.
I know I'm not a youngin'
but my ears might still be wet.
'Cause I was weaned on ol' Jim Beam.
I'm as country as it gets.

Yes, I drink Jim Beam and wear earrings.
I'm as country as it gets.

MAY 1996

Trials and Tribulations

Verse I
I'm going down to the river
watch the tide roll by.
Gonna climb up on that mountain
where the pines grow so high.

My face is bloody and lashed
from the shit that I've come through.
My soul is worn. My jeans are torn
My blood is runnin' blue.

Verse II
The clouds start to thicken.
The sun is fading fast.
The wind is freezin' cold
blowin' off my past.

Gotta find some shelter
hide me from the dark.
I think I'll lie down in my shadow,
shadow from my broken heart.

Chorus
Trials and Tribulations
Burdens dragging me down so slow
The hounds of hell are comin'
To take me where the Devil won't go.

Verse III
I've been running from the Devil
God wants me, too

I can feel the fire
I can smell the brimstone, too

If I say I'm sorry
will the Devil let go of me?
Asking for forgiveness,
will God grant me clemency?

(Guitar Solo)

BRIDGE
My mind is twisted
My back is bent
My knees hurt me so
The hounds of hell are comin'
to take me where the Devil won't go.

CHORUS II (A)
Trials and Tribulations
Time is running out
The hounds of hell are coming
Blood dripping from their mouth

CHORUS II (B)
Trials and Tribulations
Memories take their toll
Death is knockin' at my back door
To take me where the Devil won't go.

Trials and Tribulations
are all that I know.

06/09/11

I'm Going Down To Memphis

CHORUS I
I'm goin' down to Memphis,
and I gotta ride.
I'm goin' down to Memphis,
and I got me a ride.
I ain't got me no automobile,
but I got this pretty little girl right by my side.

VERSE I
This pretty little girl beside me,
She a'take me far as I wanna go.
Ride me all the way to Memphis
and keep my feet off the road.
Met her up in Detroit City,
done slid on down to the Gulf of Mexico.

CHORUS II
But, see now, I'm goin' to Memphis,
and I got to ride.
But I'm goin' to Memphis, Lord,
and I got me a ride.
I ain't got no automobile,
but got this sweet little woman,
Lord, right here by my side.

VERSE II
Don't know when I'll get there.
Don't know how long it'll take.
As long as little girl keep playin' the French harp,
Lord, I can wait.

Ain't got much time to be there,
but she make me don't care if I'm late.

(Harmonica Solo)

VERSE III
When I get to Memphis,
this little woman gonna have to set me free.
When I get to Memphis, they's just way too much I gotta see.
This little woman sweet as a Georgia peach,
but they's a tree in Tennessee.

CHORUS III
I'm going down to Memphis,
and I got me ride.
I'm going down to Memphis,
and, Lord, I had me a ride.
I ain't got no little woman no mo'.
I gots me one on each side.

JUNE, 2004

Hold Onto Your Dreams

Verse I
Life is just a rodeo,
carrying me from town to town.
Seems as soon as I leave the chute,
I wind up on the ground.
But when things get too tough
and the bull it seems too mean,
You just gotta get back on
and hold onto your dreams.

Chorus
You gotta stay in the saddle.
You gotta pull on the reins.
To make it your 8 seconds,
you gotta take some pain.
You never know what way life will take you,
but don't you get lost.
And just hold on to your dreams 'till your
dreams buck you off.

Verse II
Sometimes, you make it to the circuit,
and you get all the fame.
Sometimes, you're just the rodeo clown,
and no one knows your name.
But no matter where you wind up,
in the spotlight or in the crowd,
If you never leave the barrel,
you'll never find out.

Chorus

You gotta stay in the saddle.
You gotta pull on the reins.
To make it your 8 seconds,
you gotta take some pain.
You never know what way life will take you,
but don't you get lost.
And just hold on to your dreams 'till your
dreams buck you off.
And just hold on to your dreams 'till your
dreams buck you off.

12/26/97

WRITE TO WRITE

VERSE I
Some of write to remember;
some of us to forget,
some to ask for forgiveness,
some to express their regret.

We all try to get it right;
though, most of us rarely do.
Lots of us come off too happy,
but most of us way too blue.

CHORUS I
Well, I write to write.
Think I'll write tonight.
Bare my pen
under the pale moonlight.
Maybe a love song,
Maybe some blues,
Maybe some country,
Maybe just for you,
Maybe rock and roll,
Maybe soul,
or southern rock,
to the rhythm of this broken ol' clock.

VERSE II
I never used a metronome
or wrote sheet music to stay in time.
I have a hard enough go of it,
makin' the words continue to rhyme.

I know they don't have to,
but I guess it's just what I'm used to.
Each word painted with color:
red, green, pale yellow, or dark blue.

CHORUS II

I write to write.
Think I'll write tonight.
Put my paper to pen,
firmly but gently, like my lips upon your skin.
Hot breath down you back
like against a Shure microphone
while layin' down my latest track.
Maybe, it'll work or maybe it won't.
Sometimes it does; sometimes it don't.
Either way it goes, nobody knows
until the writer's all through
or the ink ceases to flow.

BRIDGE

I can remember the first song.
I can't remember them all.
The last one's not here yet,
but, like Waylon, I just hope
I leave with the "Belle of the Ball."

VERSE III

Writers like Tom Waits, Bob Dylan,
Ray Charles, Chris Cornell to name a few.
I write songs just for me.
And I write songs just for you.
I write them for others
with prettier voices than mine.

I know most will never make it to the radio,
the internet, or television line.

CHORUS III
At the end of it all,
I hope you'll sing along
for the words, for the tune,
for your lady, yourself, or the whole damn song.
Maybe a love song that plucks your heart strings,
as you drive down the road, headed for home.
Or a hymn like Luke the Drifter
wrote to fill and empty the pews.
Maybe it'll bring back a lover, you never wanted to lose.
A song for your mother, father, son or daughter.
Jamey Johnson said it best in one of his own,
for all those reasons "That's Why I Write Songs".
But tonight as I think and I write,
I write to write.
I just write to write.
I just write.

5/20/14

Roll, Water, Roll

CHORUS
Roll, water, roll.
Take me away,
out of this place
to a brighter day.
Roll, water, roll.
Take me on down,
out of this town.
Roll, water, roll.

VERSE I
Lord, I feel I'm sinkin'
in this great big world,
no place to call my home,
no one to call my girl,
but I can hear this river,
flowin' wild and flowin' free,
just runnin' to be runnin',
Lord, just like me.

CHORUS
Roll, water, roll.
Take me away,
out of this place
to a brighter day.
Roll, water, roll.
Take me on down,
out of this town.
Roll, water, roll.

VERSE II
Maybe, I can catch a little boat

that will let me stow away,
make it down to the Gulf of Mexico,
and drink my woes away.
I will still remember West Virginia
and its flowin' mountain streams
and the river that took me
to my blue agave dreams.

CHORUS
Roll, water, roll.
Take me away,
out of this place
to a brighter day.
Roll, water, roll.
Take me on down,
out of this town.
Roll, water, roll.

BRIDGE
Water, keep on rollin'.
Don't you ever stop.
As long as you keep on rollin',
I'll keep risin' to the top.

CHORUS
Roll, water, roll.
Take me away,
out of this place
to a brighter day.
Roll, water, roll.
Take me on down,
out of this town.
Roll, water, roll.

JULY 6, 2005

RICHARD COREY 176

It's All Gonna Come To Pass

VERSE I

Sittin' here thinkin'
Na…
I ain't even drinkin'.
I ain't smoked shit in 16 days.
I'm amazed.
I'm still driftin'
day to day,
searchin' for questions I've yet to ask.
And I know,
no matter where I go,
It's all gonna come to pass.
It's all gonna come to pass.

VERSE II

Keep on dreamin'
'bout that pot of gold.
I've looked everywhere
high and low,
searchin' for myself.
But I swear
I can't find a goddamn soul.
So what do I do,
where do I turn?
The bridges I've burned.
The traveled path,
the winding roads,
that I've yet to go.

It's all gonna come to pass.
It's all gonna come to pass.

MUSICAL BREAK

BRIDGE
The more I look,
the less I find.
The more I see,
the more I wanna be blind.

But it's all gonna come to pass.
It's all gonna come to pass.

VERSE III
I been tryin' to force it,
just tryin' to make it.
But I can't take it for one more day…
there's no way.
My destiny,
tried and true.
Lord God, my pride is black and blue…
still I ain't through.
If my cup tips over,
will ya fill my glass
with a 100 proof,
the solid truth?
It's all gonna come to pass.
Yeah, it's all gonna come to pass.

1/16/02

I Wanna Hear A Country Song

Verse I
I've ran bars, and I've stole cars
and everything in between.
Been here and there and everywhere,
there ain't much this boy ain't seen.

And I don't care if everybody stares.
I tell you there ain't nothing wrong.
Don't matter when, where, or what,
if there's an old jukebox,
I wanna hear a country song.

Chorus
So turn it up loud.
Tap your boots on the floor.
The only way in a room
is through a swinging door.
How about Alan Jackson or some old George Jones?
I wanna hear a country song.

Verse II
A steel guitar sure goes far
if you're feelin' down and out.
You can hear it in their voices. Old Hank and George,
they know what the blues are about.

When I put on my Levis, there ain't no surprise
what is going on. When I wanna two step,
it's a sure bet
I wanna hear a country song.

CHORUS
So turn it up loud.
Tap your boots on the floor.
The only way in a room
is through a swinging door.
How about Alan Jackson or some old George Jones?
I wanna hear a country song.

10/09/99

Tattoos and Scars

VERSE I
(soft guitar)
(slowly spoken with a slight singing nature)

Well, I've been knocked around some
but never finished lying on the ground.
I've seen a lot in this old world,
but I'm sure there's more to be found.

And I've been in the chair a time or two,
but I'm still not quite through.
Happy with all the ink I got
even though I had to cover up a few.

CHORUS
(faster and heavier guitar)
(sing)

Tattoos and scars are much different things,
but I wear them proudly
like a life wedding ring
because you marry'em both when you get'em.
They don't run off, and you can't forget'em.
Tattoos you pay money for, but scars they cost more.
Neither mean that you're rotten.
Yeah, tattoos and scars... I got'em.

VERSE II
(performed the same as first verse)

My tattoos you can see very clearly.
I'm not at all ashamed.

Some are covered up,
but most remain.

Most of my scars are prominent.
I nearly lost my right arm.
I reckon the mess left
takes a little away from my charm.

CHORUS
(musical break...Steel guitar and a little harder guitars)

Tattoos and scars are much different things,
but I wear them proudly
like a life wedding ring
because you marry'em both when you get'em.
They don't run off, and you can't forget'em.
Tattoos you pay money for, but scars they cost more.
Neither mean that you're rotten.
Yeah, tattoos and scars... I got'em.

BRIDGE
My tattoos aren't for show.
They're only for me.
And the scars on my soul you can't see,
but I got'em both and I have come to learn:
Tattoos you get, and the scars you earn.

(musical break harmonica and guitars w/ heavy bass)

CHORUS
Tattoos and scars are much different things,
but I wear them proudly
like a life wedding ring
because you marry'em both when you get'em.

They don't run off, and you can't forget'em.
Tattoos you pay money for, but scars they cost more.
Neither mean that you're rotten.
Yeah, tattoos and scars... I got'em.

ENDING
Somewhere I heard someone sing:
Tattoos and scars
are different things.

4/14/14

Bourbon Bound

Verse I
I tossed and I turned
After you left
And I guess
I wound up on the empty side of the bed.

I recall the sound of the door,
The smell of the perfume you wore.
And I remember
Every word that you said.

I reckon I'm off
And I know I'm lost
But I'll surely find the closest liquor store.

Or maybe a bar.
One can't be that far
And a barmaid will start to pour.

Your memory I have to drown,
'cause it keeps hanging around.
So I'm sure I'll find my way
'cause today I'm bourbon bound.

Verse II
I cracked the seal
On something from a Kentucky still
But that reminded me of your southern charms.

I held that bottle so tight
Way into the night
The way I used to hold you in my arms.

Your memory I have to drown
'cause it keeps hanging around.
The pain will show me the way.
'Cause today
I'm bourbon bound.

Chorus
So pour me a shot.
Fill it right to the top.
I need it all to erase her.
Hell no, I don't need no chaser.
I swear every drop will make it down.
Just leave the bottle.
It's her leavin' I can't swallow.
I doubt that in a fifth
A man can forget.
And I doubt I can fall in and drown.
But we'll see
'cause I'm bourbon bound.

Verse III
I'm sure there's a border
Between right and wrong ways
For me to get over you.

Meditation doesn't work.
I can't transcendentally remove the hurt.
That's why I turn to the 90 proof.

'Cause your memory I have to drown.
It keeps hanging around.
I'm sure this is a mistake, but today
I'm bourbon bound.

CHORUS

So pour me a shot.
Fill it right to the top.
I need it all to erase her.
Hell no, I don't need no chaser.
I swear every drop will make it down.
Just leave the bottle.
It's her leaving I can't swallow.
I doubt that in a fifth
A man can forget.
And I doubt I can fall in drown.
But we'll see,
'cause I'm bourbon bound.

ENDING

Your memory I have to drown.
'Cause it keeps hanging around.
This pain I just can't take.
So today, I'm bourbon bound.

11/04/03

Wish I Was There

Verse I

Livin' right on the beach.
Letting the sand tickle your feet.
Lying there reading a book.
Everyman has to take a look.

Well know it was long ago
But you have to have memories, I know
Of me and the burning sun
For a moment we were one

Chorus

I know life has passed me and you.
But, God, I wish it were true
Kissing you without coming up for air.
Wish I was there.
Yeah, I wish I was there.

Verse II

Evening comes and a glass of wine in your hand
Sittin' in the sand
watchin' the sun sink down
And just waiting for the moon to come around

Chorus

I know life has passed me and you
But, God, I wish it were true
Kissing you without coming up for air
Wish I was there.

BRIDGE

Well, I wish I was there
Holding you, The smell of your hair
And I wish I was there
To hold your hand, Love you and care
I wish I was there

VERSE III

I dream of being by your side
It wouldn't be that long of ride
Perhaps by train
Maybe by plane

CHORUS/ENDING

But I know life has passed me and you
God Damn, I wish it were true
Kissing you in the salty air
Wish I was there.

Wish…was - there.

7/27/14

You Weren't Listening At All

Verse I

Fresh out of high school, the world at my back
Just a poor ol' boy from the wrong side of the track.
A debutant beauty from west Tennessee,
I never saw what you seen in me.

Chorus

We broke free from those chains that bound us.
We tore down that great big wall,
And I longed for that day when you'd change your name.
But I guess you weren't listening at all.

Verse II

I told you I loved you, time after time,
And you said that your heart would always be mine.
I always thought that we'd be wild and free,
So how did he take your heart from me?

Chorus

We broke free from those chains that bound us.
We tore down that great big wall,
And I longed for that day when you'd change your name.
But I guess you weren't listening at all.

Verse III

Why couldn't you hear me crying?
Didn't you hear those teardrops fall?
They crashed to the ground as you walked away,
But I guess you weren't listening at all.

Chorus

We broke free from those chains that bound us.
We tore down that great big wall,
And I longed for that day when you'd change your name.
But I guess you weren't listening at all.

Verse IV

I told you I'd make music the key.
You told me always you believed in me,
But fancy clothes and cars were out of my reach.
He had it all, but he took it from me.

Chorus

We broke free from those chains that bound us.
We tore down that great big wall,
And I longed for that day when you'd change your name.
But I guess you weren't listening at all.

Chorus

We broke free from those chains that bound us.
We tore down that great big wall,
And I longed for that day when you'd change your name.
But I guess you weren't listening at all.

Maybe I wasn't listening at all.

01/28/07

Just Leave Me Alone

Verse I

There's something in my eyes.
I can barely see.
I just can't wipe enough.
I still can't see.

Running down my face
Like a mountain stream,
If you look closely,
The tears will gleam.

Chorus I

Shut the door.
Hide my face.
I am ashamed.
I'm disgraced.
Leave me alone.
I'm not answering the phone.
I'm too busy crying,
Too busy crying.
Just leave me alone.

Verse II

Think I'll head down South.
Get a couple quarts of Hemingway's whiskey.
Sit on the beach. Write a few songs.
See if anybody'd ever miss me.

The farther south I go,
The less people will know.

The salt water will make a good disguise
For these tears falling from my eyes.

CHORUS II
I wish the moon would race
Just to hide my face.
I'm ashamed.
I'm disgraced.
Not too hard to be left alone
When there is no phone.
I'm too busy crying,
Too busy crying.
Just leave me alone.

BRIDGE
Coconuts and palm trees,
A nice salty ocean breeze,
Moonlight dancing on the water,
Thoughts of my love, my son, my daughter.
Put more whiskey in my cup
Before my tears fill it up.

CHORUS III
If I fall asleep, leave me alone.
Don't wake me up till dawn.
I'm ashamed.
I'm disgraced.
Don't want no one to recognize my face.
Just leave me alone.

3/12/13

WALKING IN MY SHOES

VERSE I

I saw my ex-wife today
and I saw her brand new man.
He was holding her so tightly,
standing where I used to stand.

She took everything I had,
and I took it from her for years.
Then I noticed his shoes,
and I nearly broke down in tears.

CHORUS

He was stepping in my steps,
walking where I walked,
saying what I said,
talking what I talked.
I knew it was over.
I knew I had to lose.
He took away her heart.
But why did he take my shoes?

VERSE II

She bought me those shoes last summer.
I had only worn them once or twice.
Never gave them much thought,
but they damned sure looked nice.
I don't want her back
if she was ever mine to have.
But those shoes would be on my feet,
or they would be up his ass.

CHORUS (x 2)
He was stepping in my steps,
walking where I walked,
saying what I said,
talking what I talked.
I knew it was over.
I knew I had to lose.
He took away her heart.
But why did he take my shoes?

3/13/97

Slow Down the World

Verse I

It seems I've said some dangerous things this time.
It seems like all the judges are standing in line.
But, I don't mind.
I can't take back the things that I've said.
Sorry if I spoiled your serving of daily bread.
Heavily, I tread.

Chorus II

If I could just stop the world for a moment
see if the masses would retract their claws.
If only just for a second
the slightest pause.
Enough time for me to slow down the world
So, I can hop off.

Verse II

It seems if I've stirred up some anger and fear.
I'm not sure if anyone wants me here.
Not one tear.
You see I've got this ringing in my soul.
Once thought there was just a big ol' empty hole.
I don't know.

Chorus II

If I could just stop the world for a moment
to light a cigarette and take a couple of draws.
If only just for a second…
the slightest pause.
Enough time for me to slow down the world
so I can wander off.

BRIDGE

If you don't believe in me,
I can't make you see.
If you don't believe in me,
I can't set you free.
All I can really do… is give you a clue
You have to decide what is true.
And what is best for you.

CHORUS III/CLOSING

If I could just stop the world for a moment
bring it to a screeching halt.
Have you just listen for a second.
You can take my words with a grain of salt.
I just need a big long empty pause
so I can sneak off
maybe get lost
if I could just get - the - world - to - pause.

7/23/14

Tomorrow

CHORUS
You say,
"Wait until tomorrow."
I say, "Sure...
...there's some time I can borrow."
Tomorrow is a brand new day.
"It'll be different,"
you say.
You promise to love me and me alone.
Tomorrow...
...but tomorrow has come and gone.

VERSE I
Time is all we really need.
With enough time,
we all have a chance to proceed.
Time has been called the great healer.
But I feel like an addict waiting for his dealer.

CHORUS
You say,
"Wait until tomorrow."
I say, "Sure...
...there's some time I can borrow."
Tomorrow is a brand new day.
"It'll be different,"
you say.
You promise to love me and me alone.
Tomorrow...
...but tomorrow has come and gone.

Verse II

Love is all I've ever longed for.
I think we all have
wanted to open up that door
and be loved without condition.
But I feel like I'm suffering from an affliction.

Chorus

You say,
"Wait until tomorrow."
I say, "Sure…
…there's some time I can borrow."
Tomorrow is a brand new day.
"It'll be different,"
you say.
You promise to love me and me alone.
Tomorrow…
…but tomorrow has come and gone.

Bridge

Please, baby, I beg you
to do only what you promised me you'd do.
I would give you
a million tomorrows and then some,
if you can assure me
tomorrow will finally come.

Chorus

You say,
"Wait until tomorrow."
I say, "Sure…
…there's some time I can borrow."
Tomorrow…
…is a brand new day.

"It'll be different,"
you say.
You promised
to love me and me alone.
Tomorrow...
...but tomorrow has come and gone.

VERSE III (CLOSING)
How long must I wait?
Tell me how long,
how long will it take?
Tomorrow, Tomorrow, Tomorrow.
One more day,
then tomorrow's too late

12/27/11

How Could You Say You Love Me?

Verse I

I can remember the first time you hit me.
It hurt so bad inside.
But I never cried, I never cried.
It only got worse from there,
Kicking and pulling hair.
My soul was worse for wear.
It seemed I couldn't make it up for air.

Chorus I

But, honey, I did.
Yeah, I made it through,'
Found myself and found my voice.
And I only have one thing to say to you… Well, maybe two.
Goodbye with no tears in my eye.
And the second is a question for you.
How dare you? How Dare you?
How could you? How could you
Ever look me in the face and say the words I love you.

Verse II

I remember that November
When I finally had the courage to say to you:
Honey, we're through. Do what you wanna do.
I'm not sleeping in that bed anymore.
In fact, I won't even darken your door.
You can have the house, the furniture,
Even my TV. All I want is me
And my chance to be free.

Chorus II

Now, I'm gone.

I don't care if you're alone.
In fact, I hope you can't sleep.
I hope you can't eat.
The way you treated me,
The way you beat on me.
But it's over now so let the milk run off the table.
I'm not cryin'. In fact, I'm not able.
I wish I never said it. I fuckin' regret it.
I fucking regret it, I swear.
Every time, I wasted the air to say I love you.

BRIDGE
And how can it be, that you actually came back for me?
I don't understand why you wanted to open that door.
Because you didn't have your punching bag no more?
I guess that's why, but I don't know why you'd cry,
Let a tear touch your eyes.
So it might come as a surprise to you.
But you don't get to say I love you…. anymore.

CHORUS III
I'm gone. You don't deserve a goodbye.
No hug. No kiss. Not even the right to miss me.
You know all the reasons why,
So don't you say it. Don't let it cross your lips.
So don't you say it. Don't let it cross your lips.
Poison from your mouth and a rabid tooth
Never could tell the truth, and the difference she couldn't see.
How could you have ever looked me in the face
And say you love me, you love me, you love me?
How could you say you love me?

2/16/13

I Fell Again

Verse I
I fell for you, sometime ago.
It seems like forever, I know.
Just the same, it feels like only yesterday.
Perhaps it was or maybe I should say,
"Yesterday, my best friend,
I fell again."

No one knows me like you do.
No one ever will. I only open up for you.
Is it really us in love or only me?
I'm tied to you, but you are free.
Is it love or is it sin?
Regardless, I fell again.

Chorus
I fell again,
and I keep falling.
I still answer,
and you keep calling.
So it just can't be me, can it?
You tell me you don't love him.
And I fell again.

Verse II
Love is such a sticky game to play.
Right or wrong, who can really say?
She loves me, she loves me not.
I'm all tied up in a million knots.
You say your mine and have always been.
And I fell again.

BRIDGE

Again and again,
I keep falling.
Again and again,
You keep stalling.
But you promise
we are more than friends.
And I fell again.

VERSE III

How I long to hold your hand.
Beside you, I long to stand.
I want to whisper in your ear
everything I love, everything I fear.
You say you want that too,
and for it never to end,
and I fell again.

CHORUS

I fell again,
and I keep falling.
I cry myself to sleep.
Can you hear me calling?
You say it's not just me.
Your tears are falling too.
And I fell again for you.

I swear it's true.
Every day I fall again, in love with you.

12/21/11

WHY DID YOU DO THIS TO ME?

VERSE I
I thought we had it all,
but I guess it wasn't enough.
You thought our marriage was based on business.
I thought it was trust.

I thought we made a perfect pair,
but you threw us away.
You made a perfect bluff
on our wedding day.

CHORUS
'Cause you made me love you, then you said goodbye.
All you left was a note and a teardrop in my eye.
It said that you love me, but you needed to be free.
Why did you do this to me?

VERSE II
It could have been a lot worse.
You could have taken everything,
but you only took my heart.
You even left your wedding ring.

You left me all the silver
and all the pictures we had.
I feel entitled to be angry,
but, honey I'm not mad.

CHORUS
'Cause you made me love you, then you said goodbye.
All you left was a note and a teardrop in my eye.

It said that you love me, but you needed to be free.
Why did you do this to me?

HOOK
Why did you do this to me?
Did I not love you enough?
I think now I got it wrong.
Why did you do this to us?

CHORUS
'Cause you made me love you, then you said goodbye.
All you left was a note and a teardrop in my eye.
It said that you love me, but you needed to be free.
Why did you do this to me?
Oh, why did you do this to me?

4/13/11

A Long Night

VERSE I

I always talk to you
before I lie down to sleep.
Instead of the Lord,
I pray for you my soul to keep.
But something's wrong,
something ain't quite right.
You didn't call.
It's gonna be a long night.
Yeah, it's gonna be a long night.

VERSE II

The last time we talked
the conversation went up and down,
like all conversations always do
but this one left me with a frown.
Lying here writing by candlelight.
That's all I need
'cause it's gonna be a long night.
Yeah, it's gonna be a long night.

CHORUS

It's gonna be a long, long night;
peering through these tears,
leering in the shadows,
shaking from the rain and fears.
I'm sure I'll be all right,
it's just gonna be a long night.
Yeah, I'm gonna have a long night.

VERSE III

Just a word from you
bad or good,
misheard or misunderstood.
Anything would be fine
if I could just hear you smile.
Would sure take some time
off of this long night.
I think it's gonna be a long night.

CHORUS

It's gonna be a long, long night;
peering through these tears,
leering in the shadows,
shaking from the rain and fears.
I'm sure I'll be all right,
it's just gonna be a long night.
Yeah, I'm gonna have a long night.

ENDING

I'm sorry I've lost my ring,
I can't seem to sing
or find the words to the song.
Be careful going home.
I'm sorry about the long drive
and sorry about the long night.
I'm sorry about this long night.

8/27/11

I Don't Share

I was born an only child,
So I never really learned to share.
Maybe, I was hard to play with.
I used to cut off my girlfriend's dolly's hair.

But I wasn't being mean.
I just wanted her attention.
I only wanted her to play with me.
And if I forgot to mention:

I don't share.

The older I got,

It never got any better.
A teacher took and note I passed,
And said get up in front of the class
and read this letter.

So I got up and took the note,
Held it in my hand.
And as he lay on the ground.
I said, "Maybe you don't understand.

I don't share."

I'm not all selfish.
Don't get the wrong impression.
I'd give a stranger the shirt right off my back.
Giving ain't quite the same thing if you ain't learned that lesson.

I don't share.

They tell me I'm all grown up now,
And I shouldn't act the way I do.
They say I should share my wealth.
That's what Jesus would do.

Buddy, why don't you get off my back?
Me and Jesus are just fine,
And you better stop looking at my woman like that
'Cause, brother, she is mine.

And I don't share.

I don't' share my emotions.
I don't share my food.
I don't share my favorite blanket.
I don't mean to be rude.

I just don't share.

Maybe, I'll get better
As I get more grey.
Just keep your hands of my whisky and woman.
Didn't you hear me say?

I don't share.
I might burn in hell because of it,
But I don't really care.
I don't share.

2/12/11

I'm Diggin' Your Grave

CHORUS I
I'm a diggin' your grave
I'm a diggin' your grave
With a silver spoon
With a silver spoon
I'm a diggin' your grave
With a silver spoon
By the light of the moon
I'm a diggin your grave

VERSE I
You were a devil, as sure as Hell
You were a devil, everyone knew well
You were a thief.
You were a cheat.
Now you're lyin' in a grave not too deep.
You're in a grave 'bout 2 feet deep.

CHORUS I
I'm a diggin' your grave
I'm a diggin' your grave
With a silver spoon
With a silver spoon
I'm a diggin your grave
With a silver spoon
By the light of the moon
I'm a diggin your grave

VERSE II
You came a creepin' round my door.
You came a creepin' round about 4.

You were a lookin' for somethin' to steal,
Something to sell to buy you a pill.
My mother's silver is what you found.
Now one a them spoons is puttin' you in the ground.

CHORUS II
I'm a diggin your grave
I'm a diggin your grave
With a silver spoon you tried to steal
With a silver spoon you tried to steal
I'm a diggin your grave
With a silver spoon
About 2 feet deep
The Devil will come
for you soon.

BRIDGE
The devil's waiting / for you my friend
Maybe what I did / was a sin
But a thief / goes straight to Hell
I saw the demons / as you fell

VERSE III
I shot you right in the head
I ain't sorry that you are dead
Maybe I will see you when I die
For shootin' you betwixt the eyes
You ain't worthy of a place in Hell
When you answer what lie will you tell?

CHORUS III / ENDING
Now I'm a diggin' your grave
I'm a diggin' your grave
With a silver spoon

With a silver spoon
I'm a diggin' your grave
With a silver spoon
I'm a diggin' your grave
By the light of the moon
I'm a diggin' your grave
I'm...diggin' - your - g-r-a-v-e.

8/15/14

A Lie Is A Lie Is A Lie

Verse I

Baby, sometimes in my mind,
I can't keep things quite straight.
And, when I stand in the judgment line
At the end of time, I may not make it through the pearly gates.
But I don't care because, Baby, I swear
If I don't make it through,
It won't be because I lied to you.

Verse II

Baby, I never lied.
If I would've, maybe we may not have cried as much.
But you deserved the truth,
About everything, not just you.
Maybe, I was wrong; sometimes, the truth just belongs to us.
Maybe, I was wrong; maybe, I was right.
But the right may not be the truth,
I just can't lie to you.

Chorus

'Cause when the truth hurts
Maybe, it's just not worth it.
'Cause when the truth hurts,
Maybe, we don't deserve it.
'Cause hurt is hurt whether it's wrong, right, false, or true.
And, my love, I would never intentionally hurt you.

Verse III

Baby, there was never anything to lie about.
But there were some things that never should have left my mouth.
Some things are just better left unspoken

Even when they are for the most part jokin'.
When things are left unsaid,
Up until the time we're dead.
That's sometimes for the best when things are left unsaid.

Chorus
'Cause when the truth hurts
Maybe, it's just not worth it.
'Cause when the truth hurts,
Maybe, we don't deserve it.
'Cause hurt is hurt whether it's wrong, right, false, or true.
And, my love, I would never intentionally hurt you.
And, maybe, I believe you would never lie to me.

I believe… No, I'm sure… You would never lie to me.

3/14/13

Chasing Shadows

VERSE I

An illusion can cause so much confusion.
Like yesterday, I could swear I saw you.
But, like a shooting star, you just faded away.
You were eaten up by the night sky. No reason why.
You disappeared, or maybe you were never there.
I don't know. It's been so long.
Should I care? You're already gone.

CHORUS

How do we know who to love?
Do we wait for answers from above?
How do I know who to let love me?
It's like chasing shadows.
They're there then gone.
Like chasing shadows,
What happens when the lights come on?
Are they there? Are they gone?
Have they simply moved along the floor or the wall?
Chasing shadows.
Were they ever really there at all?

VERSE II

Not a note. Not a sign. Were you just a figment of my mind?
Like last night, I could swear I saw you.
But like a moth, you just fluttered away.
Behind the clouds the moonlight simply fades.
You were gone, but you have been for years.
I can't see through all these damn tears.

CHORUS

How do we know who to love?
Do we wait for answers from above?
How do I know who to let love me?
Simple answers we cannot see.
How can we know?
It's like chasing shadows.
They're there, then gone.
It's like chasing shadows.
What happens when the lights come on?
Are they there? Are they gone?
Have they simply moved along the floor or wall?
Chasing shadows. Were they really there at all?

BRIDGE

You can reach out and even touch their hand.
But you can't hold them or ever understand.
Who cares? Who knows? They come. They go.
Shadows…

CHORUS

How do we know who to love?
Do we wait for answers from above?
How do I know who to let love me?
Simple answers we cannot see.
How can we know?
It's like chasing shadows.
They're there, then gone.
It's like chasing shows.
What happens when the lights come on?
Are they there? Are they gone?
Have they simply moved along the floor or wall?

Chasing shadows. Were they really there at all?
Chasing shadows.
Shadows.

5/18/12

Melting Away

Verse I
I know
how you love the snow.
I see your face
in every flake.
Your heart makes this sound
when the snow hits the ground.
Your eyes glimmer
when the snow shimmers.
Your warm up my soul
despite the cold,
my angel in the snow.
No need for a halo.
Warming me up, like a cup of cocoa.

Chorus
Melting away like a block of ice
around my heart.
Drip dropping everyday
from the start.
I don't know why
I try to fight.
I cry
everyday we're apart.
Look inside my eyes
through to my soul,
and your reflection
in the puddle
surrounding my heart.

VERSE II

I don't understand
the appeal of the snowman.
I'll try to see
if you build one with me.
No need for fire,
I burn with desire.
We'll lay on the ground
and watch it fall down.
Tell you I love you
without making a sound.

CHORUS

Melting away like a block of ice
around my heart.
Drip dropping everyday
from the start.
I don't know why
I try to fight.
I cry
everyday we're apart.
Look inside my eyes
through to my soul,
and your reflection
in the puddle
surrounding my heart.

PIANO BRIDGE

CHORUS

Melting away like a block of ice
around my heart.
Drip dropping everyday
from the start.

I don't know why
I try to fight.
I cry
everyday we're apart.
Look inside my eyes
through to my soul,
and your reflection
in the puddle
surrounding my heart.

You surround my heart.

9/13/13

BABY, I'M SORRY

VERSE I

I knew I was wrong,
When I didn't make it home
On Tuesday till a quarter to four.
You'd already changed the lock on the door.
And all I found was a black penned note
That said: You don't live here anymore.
I'm not gonna lie. To hell with my pride,
I sat on that porch, and I cussed and I cried.
And I ran away. Yeah, I ran away.

VERSE II

At first, I thought I'd lost my mind.
I bought two bags of ice, the Polar Bear kind,
A couple cases of Bud, and took off to the woods.
I've been sleeping in the mud, Baby. I ain't doin' no good.
In every star I see, I see your eyes.
I get all balled up and start to cry.
What can I do
To get a tear out of you?
And I wonder…yeah, I wonder.

CHORUS

What if I called you up
And told you I was sorry, baby?
Would you hang up the phone
Or ask me to come home, baby?
Could we talk all night
Or would we fuss and fight, baby?
I would do anything just to make this right.
Baby, I'm sorry.

Verse III

You said once before,
"I was your light in a storm."
You have to know it's the same for me,
You're my anchor in the roughest sea.
I never meant to push your heart aside.
Your love is the strongest thing I've tried.
I never meant to let our love drown.
Never again will I let you down.
Baby, baby, toss a rope to me.

Bridge

Yeah, Baby, I was wrong.
I belong at home beside you, beside you.
Anything you need, I'll lay it down at your feet.
Please believe me. Yeah, believe me when I say I'm sorry.

(Guitar solo with a little piano and big drum finish)

Chorus

What if I called you up
And told you I was sorry, baby?
Would you hang up the phone
Or ask me to come home, baby?
Could we talk all night
Or would we fuss and fight, baby?
I would do anything just to make this right.
Baby, I'm sorry.
Baby, I'm sorry.

9/8/13

I Am Alive

VERSE I

Livin' outta suitcase.
Pocket full of danger.
Ordered to kill
a blue-eyed stranger.

A la carte blood kisses
with an extra shot of poison.
Locked in the mind's attic,
A place to keep my toys in.

CHORUS

Welcome me back
to the land of the living.
Gonna eat the world
Absolutely no forgiving.
It's great to be back.
No one thought I'd survive.
Welcome me back.
I am alive.

VERSE II

Met the devil at the cross roads
and made my deal.
You may not believe me,
but the devil is real.

Smokin' hot red lips
And a Suicide kiss,
I crossed the devil
And got my wish.

CHORUS

Welcome me back
to the land of the living.
Gonna eat the world
Absolutely no forgiving.
It's great to be back
no one thought I'd survive.
Welcome me back
I am alive.

BRIDGE
(almost poem like…)
I can't help you understand
how I got back
from the fiery land.
From underneath
the devil's right hand,
I made my choice
Became a man.
Stared down the devil
her pretty blue eyes
She is dead.
And I am alive!

(Guitar and Dulcimer solos)

CHORUS

Welcome me back
to the land of the living.
Gonna eat the world
absolutely no forgiving.
It's great to be back
no one thought I'd survive.

Welcome me back
I am alive.

(tinny piano solo…)

I am alive.
I am alive.
I am alive.

12/26/11

No More Life To Live

Verse I

Please tell my momma that I'm sorry.
You see, I was her only child.
I've walked a road of sorrow.
I just can't make it another mile.

Tell my daddy I couldn't make it.
I just couldn't take it another day.
I know you're sick and on your way.
I gotta go first. I can't put you in no grave.

Chorus I

You can call me a quitter.
You can call me whatever you want.
You can call me selfish.
No one will defend me.
I don't have too many friends.
You can call me a sinner or grin
As my ashes take hold to the wind.

Verse II

I got a couple of children,
But I don't think they'll miss me when I'm gone.
I've never been much of a father.
Don't imagine it will hurt them for too long.

And then, baby, there's you,
The only thing I've held on to.
I know you won't like it.
Don't know if you'll be mad or sad or blue.

Chorus II

You can call me what you wish:
A coward, a bastard, a son of a bitch.
But you don't know how hard it is
To let go.
Got this gun pointed at my head.
In just one second, I'll be dead.

Chorus I

You can call me a quitter.
You can call me whatever you want.
You can call me selfish.
No one will defend me.
I don't have too many friends.
You can call me a sinner or just grin
As my ashes take hold to the wind.

4/11/13

It's All My Fault

VERSE I
I sit alone at this table
Created for four,
Realizing that there's no one
But me on this floor.

Cigarette smoke fills my head,
Clouds my eyes.
Peer through the darkness
As I die inside.

CHORUS
I take a step back.
Look what I've done.
I take a step back.
The pain I have caused.
I take a step back
And realize… .

It's all my fault.
Yeah, it's all my fault.

VERSE II
The blood's on my hands,
A permanent stain.
Lies and deception,
The name of the game.

The torture of the world
I know so well.
The cross that I bear
Leads me to hell.

RICHARD COREY 228

Chorus

I take a step back.
Look what I've done.
I take a step back.
The pain I have caused.
I take a step back
And realize... .

It's all my fault.
Yeah, it's all my fault.

Bridge

I can't feel.
I can't touch.
I can't love.
I can't breathe.
I can't die.
I can't lie.

Chorus

I take a step back.
Look what I've done.
I take a step back.
The pain I have caused.
I take a step back
And realize... .

It's all my fault.
Yeah, it's all my fault.

7/25/2000

REGRET

VERSE I
I don't know what I did
to upset the man upstairs.
It must have been pretty bad
'cause he's been taking it out on me for years.
Was it the weed, the whiskey, the women,
or the wine?
Lord, please tell me what I did
so I can serve my time.

CHORUS
Well, I know I've drunk
and I've smoked,
told some dirty jokes,
and I've cussed, and I've lied.
But now, I'm broken down inside.
So if you're listening up there, Lord,
place your last bet.
You've got yourself a winner
if you put your money on my regret.

VERSE II
I wish I could take it all back,
Undo the things I've done.
But things don't work that way,
at least not where I come from.
I guess I could run and hide,
maybe break down and cry.
Lord, please tell me what to do.
I won't be a beggar; I'll pay my dues.

CHORUS

Well, I know I've drunk
and I've smoked,
told some dirty jokes,
and I've cussed, and I've lied.
But now, I'm broken down inside.
So if you're listening up there, Lord,
place your last bet.
You've got yourself a winner
if you put your money on my regret.

BRIDGE

I guess you're not a betting man.
But you gotta like the odds
'cause I regret damn near everything,
even what I forgot.

CHORUS

Well, I know I've drunk
and I've smoked,
told some dirty jokes,
and I've cussed, and I've lied.
But now, I'm broken down inside.
So if you're listening up there, Lord,
place your last bet.
You've got yourself a winner
if you put your money on my regret.

ENDING

Someone throw me a net.
I'm drowning in my regret,
drowning in my regret.

7/7/05

Don't Ask Me Why

It has become so hard to swallow.
This has all but left me hollow.
I can't stand to face tomorrow.
My time here is only borrowed.

My thoughts are all mistaken.
My barren soul has left me aching.
Dreams and hopes have been taken.
A cold black heart, my body's shaking.

Chorus (Part One)
Kick me. Beat me.
I can take it.
I'm so used to it by now.
Rape me. Kill me.
It's got to end somehow.

Chorus (Part Two)
I can't live. I can't die.
I don't want to survive
in this life.
Just don't ask me why. Don't ask me why.

Verse Two
Fears and anger control my mind.
Self-pity has left me in such a bind.
Pieces of me I cannot find.
Bury me. Could you be so kind?

Chorus
Kick me. Beat me.

I can take it.
I'm so used to it by now.
Rape me. Kill me.
It's got to end somehow.

CHORUS (PART TWO)
I can't live. I can't die.
I don't want to survive
in this life.
Just don't ask me why. Don't ask me why.

(MUSICAL BRIDGE)

(CHORUS PART TWO ONLY)

Don't ask me why.

5/15/02

Go It Alone

Oh my God, let me die.
I don't want a bigger piece of the pie.
Oh my God, let me in.
My back is bowed from the burden of sin.

Red Rum, Red Rum
Motherfuckers!
Red Rum, Red Rum
Son of a bitch!
Red Rum, Red Rum
Little children
Red Rum, Red Rum
Piled in a ditch!

Take it all, take me home.
A man can't walk on broken bones.
Take me in; let it begin.
My mind is twisted, broken, and bent.

Red Rum, Red Rum
Stand to be judged!
Red Rum, Red Rum
Don't give a shit!
Red Rum, Red Rum
Adolescents!
Red Rum, Red Rum
Fuck you. I quit!

Oh my God, here I come.
Tell St. Peter I'm bringing a gun.

Oh my God, let me pass.
Devil dogs are on my ass!

Red Rum, Red Rum
Fuck mankind!
Red Rum, Red Rum
Let'em burn!
Red Rum, Red Rum
Russian roulette!
Red Rum, Red Rum
It's your turn.

Oh my God, what's the deal?
No money, all skill!
Oh my God, are you mad at me?
You keep pushing me down when I climb your tree!

Red Rum, Red Rum
Fuck Stephen King!
Red Rum, Red Rum
Fuck these dreams!
Red Rum, Red Rum
Fuck if I care!
Red Rum, Red Rum
Fighting for air!

Oh my God, on my knees.
How many more ways can I say please?
Oh my God, head in my hands.
I keep looking for the promised land.
Oh my God, I'm so low.
Keeps on raining but my river won't flow.
Oh my God!
Oh my God!

Oh my God!
Damn it to hell!
Son of a bitch!

1/23/13

THE SPIDER LADY

Hey, girl, I never saw you comin'.
You took me by surprise.
You crept up and caught me like a spider
with a blood lust, boiling in your eyes.

Do you really want me, baby?
Can you say it with a straight face?
Don't leave me hanging 'round your web
too long, just taking up space.

Hey, girl, I can see you watching me
from across this empty room.
Sweep me up, you wicked little woman,
with your deadly witch's broom.

Did you cast a spell on me, baby?
Tell me if your magic's true.
Did you enchant my heart?
I can only think of you.

I can only think of you
when the moon shines through
the clouds in the midnight sky.

Tell me the truth.
Give me some proof.
Baby, don't you lie.

Hey, girl, I know you hear me callin',
But are you listening?
Believe me, lady, there's a difference.
Are you lips glistening?

Is your heart pounding, baby?
Would I make your dreams come true?
I have no idea what I'm doin'.
I can only think of you.

I can only think of you,
or so it seems.
You haunt me in my dreams.

Do I get your blood a' going
like a fountain flowing?
Do you only think of me?

Hey, girl, do you really want me?

3/18/2011

A Little More Everyday

Verse I
It's a cold world
that I've been living in.
Dark shadows
chasing me through every sin.
Nowhere to hide,
too weak to run.
Scared of the moon.
Terrified of the sun.

Chorus I
But when you hold me
and when you kiss me,
the fear just fades away.
No need to hide from the moonlight.
The sunlight now warms my heart,
a little more every day.
So whisper softly, what you need to say.
I'll grow stronger, hold you longer
a little more every day.
A little more every day.

Verse II
This world never wanted me.
Ever since I was a kid,
danger around each corner,
death in everything I did.
Too proud to run.
Too proud to hide.
I was meant to find you
or I would've died.

Chorus II

When you hold me,
I finally feel safe.
I feel much stronger.
I finally found faith.
Faith in life.
Faith in you.
Love grows stronger,
love so true.
You lead me through the wilderness.
You show me the way…
a little more every day.
A little more every day.

Bridge

A little more every day,
you teach me how to love,
you teach me why to pray.
You help me get stronger
a little more every day.
Just a little more every day.

Chorus

Hold me, baby.
Whisper in my ear
that you love me.
Say it clear.
Make my heartbeat.
Clear my head with what you say.
I will love you.
A little more every day.
A little more every day.

11/14/12

FACEBOOK ROMANCE

CHORUS
It's just a Facebook romance,
never meant to be
accepted by no one
except for you and me.
It's just a Facebook romance.

VERSE I
I can't remember how it started,
But I know I messaged you.
You looked so beautiful
from your profile view.

I must have said "hello"
or maybe "how are you".
I can't believe I fell so easy;
now you love me too

CHORUS
It's just a Facebook romance,
never meant to be
accepted by no one
except for you and me.
It's just a Facebook romance.

VERSE II
I love logging on
And your picture is on my left.
I ask if we can talk.
Then I see a smiley face and a yes.

LOL I'm so glad that you're on.
Technology brought us together,
But it's you that turns me on.

CHORUS
It's just a Facebook romance,
never meant to be
accepted by no one
except for you and me.
It's just a Facebook romance.

BREAK
Daily phone calls.
Daily emails.
Call me at home
or try me on my cell.

CHORUS
It's just a Facebook romance,
never meant to be
accepted by no one
except for you and me.
It's just a Facebook romance.

This is so sweet.
Now were gonna meet.

It's just a Facebook romance.
It's just a Facebook romance.

4/13/11

Believe

Verse I
How can you tell
this is the beginning or the end
of the world for me?

How are you willing
to risk or persist
that we can make it through this world of hypocrisy?

I guess there's really
just one answer that I need:
Do you believe in me?

Verse II
I guess you wonder how
I can tell you're more
than a drop in a wishing well for me.

I'm willing to risk
everything that I am, that I have,
that you're more than just a fantasy.

On my life,
I swear it's true
because I believe
in you.

Chorus
To believe
is all we really need.
I believe in you
if you believe in me.

It's true.
No proof, just truth,
is all we need…
Believe.

Verse II
All my life,
all I've wanted
seems to lie in you.

I could be wrong.
But I'll be strong
for you.

I guess there's really
just one answer that I need.
Do you believe
in me?

Bridge
Do you believe?
Do you have to see?
Can't we just agree?
That's all we need
is you and me,
to believe.

Verse IV
Can you swear
you care?
Care enough
to be there?
Through the good
and bad…

I will kiss you, when you're happy.
I will hold you, when you're sad.
All I need
is for you to believe
in me.

Chorus
To believe
is all we really need.
I believe in you
if you believe in me.
It's true.
No proof, just truth
is all we need.
Believe.

Just Believe.

5/17/14

Away, Away, Away

Verse I
I feel bottled up inside.
I feel like I just need to run away.
Maybe take a Spanish holiday,
or just start running for the border down to Mexico.
Either one would be fine with me as long as you tell me that you
will go.
We'll get a bottle of tequila and a bottle of rum,
And lay around and soak up the agave sun.
How does that sound to you?
I can pick you up around a quarter till two.

Verse II
We'll drive, drive, drive
until we can smell the water and feel the sand.
Then we'll sell the car and rent us a hut on the beach.
We'll have to keep it quiet, but the bed won't squeak.
Lobster for breakfast, caught by hand.
Tacos in the evening from a little taco stand.
Dancing under the stars.
Look, baby, that one's Venus and that one's Mars.
Just waiting for the sun,
each ray carrying a ton of fun.
Send your family a postcard, baby.
Tell'em how much fun it is in Mexico,
and you think everyone should go.
Tell'em 'hello' from me,
that's all I have to say.
I gotta get back to our holiday.
Away, away, away.

Verse III

When the mariachis get to0 much to stand,
we'll start hiking down that stretch of sand.
I've always wanted to see Brazil.
How does that sound? How do you feel?
We're in South America, where we can get drugs with ease.
We can stay awake chewing on coca leaves or smoke some pot to
get some sleep.
When we get to Brazil, we'll shed our clothes on the beach.
And at night we'll drink at a bar and practice Portuguese.

Verse IV

We'll swim, swim, swim.
Baby, all night long.
We'll swim, swim, swim
with nothing on.
We'll watch the sun come up on an island off the mainland.
Lie naked in the sun and keep working on our tans.
Crack the top on the tequila and have us some shots.
Before we make it to the worm, we'll smoke some more pot.
Alone with you on an island has always been my dream.
With you by my side, this holiday is heaven, it seems.
Away, away, away.

Verse V

We'll have to hop a steamer and be stowaways.
Wherever it goes, baby, is where we'll stay.
Maybe we'll end up in Spain, where the sangria bathes our brains.
Or maybe we'll hit Sicily,
and we'll get so tangled in linguini that we'll never get free.
Maybe we'll land in Greece where we can dive for the sponge,
and let the yogurt cool off our tongues.
On our holiday: away, away, away.

Verse VI

Well, the steamer made land back in the states.
St. Simons Island is our final break.
Mimosas in the morning to drink
And a walk down the beach to help us think.
Do we wanna stay here or do we wanna go home?
It's up to you 'cause with you is where I belong.
With you is always a holiday.
Away, away, away.

Your kiss takes me away, away, away.

8/12/13

I Can Feel You

VERSE I
With a wounded heart I pray tonight,
Wishin' and hopin' that you're alright
'Cause you're so far away,
So far away.

I can't wait for the day
That you come home so I can hear you say,
"I love you. I love you more."

CHORUS I
I can smell you on my pillow.
I can taste you in my wine.
But I can't hold on to your pictures.
I can't touch you in my mind.
But I can feel you… in my heart.
Yes, I can feel you… in my heart.

VERSE II
Thoughts of you dance in my head
As I lie awake in this empty bed
Cause you're so far away,
So far away.

CHORUS II
I can see you in my dreams.
I can hear you in my song.
But I can't kiss your lips goodnight,
Or wake up to you at dawn.
But I can feel you… in my heart.
Yes, I can feel you… in my heart.

BRIDGE
I can feel you in my heart.
I can feel you in my bones.
I can feel you in my soul.
Our love goes on and on.

CLOSING
Yes, I can feel you... in my heart.
Yes, I can feel you... In my heart.

1/31/01

'CAUSE YOU LOVE ME

VERSE I

When I step on the stage, I have a voice.
I only step off because I have no choice.
When the show is all over, I forget who I am,
Lost in translation no one understands.

I walk with my head hung down in shame.
People know who I am, but they don't know my name.
The parts I played no one will forget,
But my best role of all hasn't started yet.

CHORUS

And I am who I am 'cause you make me be.
I love how I love 'cause you make me see.
I fly like I fly 'cause you set me free.
But I live 'cause you love me.

VERSE II

I have tried all my life to be special.
Against the tide of the ocean, I could not pull.
I looked everywhere, but I could not find
Any piece of me, any peace of mind.

Searching for answers in demons' dreams,
I won't get out alive or so it seems.
The curtain is down. Am I out of luck?
I turn to leave, but the lights come up.

CHORUS

And I am who I am 'cause you make me be.
I love how I love 'cause you make me see.

I fly like I fly 'cause you set me free.
But I live 'cause you love me.

BRIDGE
Now I see clearly.
All the edges defined.
With my heart, I've paid dearly.
But all the reward is all mine.

CHORUS
And I am who I am 'cause you make me be.
I love how I love 'cause you make me see.
I fly like I fly 'cause you set me free.
But I live 'cause you love me.

But I live… 'cause you love me.
You love me.

4/15/11

Not Even Shakespeare Knows

VERSE I

There's a lot of ways to say it
and a lot of ways to play it
on the big screen.
A black and white old movie
just can't seem to move me
after all the love I've seen.
I just don't know how to show it.
I'm so afraid to blow it
and, baby, you're my everything.

CHORUS

So, baby, hold on tight.
Let's turn out the light
and I'll hold you close.
I love you so much.
Can't you feel it in my touch?
Maybe, I'll try poetry or prose.
I can't find the words.
Perhaps, it's my nerves.
And after all my research,
I found out
not even Shakespeare knows.

VERSE II

I never used to mind being alone.
Now, I can't stand it when you're gone
for just a little while.
I know that you'll soon be back,
but it feels just like a heart attack
when I can't see your smile.

I just can't express it,
no matter how you undress it.
Baby, my love's on trial.
I'm guilty of love in the first degree.
That's all that's wrong with me;
just wish I could make you see.

CHORUS
So, baby, hold on tight.
Let's turn out the light
and I'll hold you close.
I love you so much.
Can't you feel it in my touch?
Maybe, I'll try poetry or prose.

I can't find the words.
Perhaps, it's my nerves.
And after all my research,
I found out
not even Shakespeare knows.

BRIDGE
I guess Frost got lost
down that road less traveled by.
Old Hemingway must have gotten too high.
Not the ringing of the bells
from Edgar Allan Poe.
None of these great poets
can say how much I love you,
not even Shakespeare knows.

CHORUS
So, baby, hold on tight.
Let's turn out the light

and I'll hold you close.
I love you so much.
Can't you feel it in my touch?
Maybe, I'll try poetry or prose.
I can't find the words.
Perhaps, it's my nerves.
And after all my research,
I found out.
not even Shakespeare knows.

Closing
I can't seem to show it.
I guess that's the way love goes.
And not even Shakespeare knows.
Not even Shakespeare knows.

12/21/12

Not A Minute Too Soon

VERSE I
Please don't let your head hang down, Baby.
And, darling, please don't cry.
I know the world hurts you, Baby,
but I will always be by your side.

Take my hand and we'll fly away
through the clouds and hide in the sky.
Only God will be able to find us,
And it will only rain when we cry.

CHORUS I
The world can't hurt us when we're together.
When we make love, the sun will shine.
Hiding in the clouds lets us control the weather.
I am yours and you are mine,
covered by a blanket on the moon.
Singing you to sleep with this little tune.
We can never leave too soon.
Never too soon.

VERSE II
I know you're scared. I can see it in your eyes.
Baby, I am too. That should be no surprise.
Waiting on that old mission bell,
Waiting for it to ring,
so we can leave, leave everything.
Head down an old border road.
Where we are headed, only the Lord knows.

Chorus II

The darkness is calling, but it can't hurt us.
The light we create will never desert us.
Tickets in hand for that magic train,
that magic train to freedom with a layover in Spain,
so the sangria can drown our pain on this trip.
Magic train and flying ship to the moon.
We can never leave too soon.
Never too soon.

Bridge

Never too soon to leave this fuckin' place.
We'll shine like a new dime once we wash our face.
The breeze is calling, no more tears falling.
Once we escape, once we break free,
and then we will see and hear this little tune.
We can never leave too soon.
Never too soon.

Chorus III

Don't stop; don't dare look back.
We've left nothing behind us.
We have everything in our hobo's sack.
Not a peek, not a glance
no toll for us 'cause God ain't got no pockets in his pants.
Set up house in a magical balloon.
There will be plenty of room.
We can never leave too soon.
Not a minute too soon.
Not a minute too soon.

12/19/12

I'll Do Anything for You

VERSE I
I'll bring you flowers every day.
I'll even pick'em in the rain.
I'll cry for you each night
till the rivers flood with pain.
I'll walk a million miles
just to get to you
'cause when it comes to our love,
there's nothing' I won't do.

CHORUS
I'll do anything
to show you how I feel.
I'll do anything
to prove my love is real.
Try to make you happy, never sad, never blue.
I'll do anything.
I'll do anything for you.

VERSE II
I know that I'm not perfect.
I can't do everything right.
But I'll do my best to love you,
kiss you good morning and good night.
You'll never feel less than special.
Baby, that's the truth.
Our love is forever.
We'll be the living proof.

CHORUS
I'll do anything
to show you how I feel.

RICHARD COREY 258

I'll do anything
to prove my love is real.
Try to make you happy, never sad, never blue.
I'll do anything.
I'll do anything for you.

10/97

Guide Me There

Verse I
This road I've chosen
seems to be leading me nowhere.
Running fast
hiding from my sin,
I have no idea where I'm heading,
and the leaves cover up where I've already been.
So what to do?
Do I stop here?
What is my motivation?
Is it fate, philosophy, or fear?

Chorus I
Could you help me out?
Could you take my hand?
Help me stand, be a man.
Let me know you care
and just let me be near you.
Guide me there.

Verse II
I've tried to use my moral compass,
but it always says I'm wrong.
I've tried to follow the sunlight
and the north star when it's gone.
Do I turn right?
Or take what's left?
What is my motivation?
Is it life love or death?

Chorus II

Could you drop a hint?
Could you drop a line?
Help me change or help me make up my mind.
Let me know you care
and just let me be near you.
Guide me there.

Break

I don't want much,
just someone to love,
someone to love me,
just to feel your touch.
Your soft lips,
your sweet kiss,
the smell of your hair
as it falls around me.
Guide me there.
Guide me there.

Verse III

The path less traveled
seems to have led me astray.
If I would've, should've, or could've been,
would I still be here today?
Wanting you.
Needing you.
My heart beating you.
What's my motivation?
I only want to be with you.

Chorus III

Could you draw me a map?
Give me a direction?

To touch your face,
redden your complexion.
Let me know you care.
Guide me there.
With you is the only place I wanna be.
Guide me there.
Guide me there.
With you… with me.

10/26/11

Out To Please

Verse I
The day we first kissed,
girl, I knew it was true.
I looked in your eyes,
and you looked in mine, too.
Each day after that, it became so much more.
I longed to touch your body, girl, like never before.
So please don't deny me. Don't make me beg.
Let me kiss all over your body.
"Let's start wit dat leg!"

Chorus
Let me caress you, hold you so tight,
making' love to ya, baby, all through the night.
Nibble on your ear, taste your lips,
making magic, girl, as I squeeze your hips.
Let your hair fall all around me, don't care if you tease.
Cause, baby, it's you that I'm out to please.

Verse II
Never before have I felt like this.
I don't believe it started from just a kiss.
Oh baby, baby, don't know what to say.
I'm so into ya girl,
"Ain't nuttin' gettin'
in my way."

Chorus
Let me caress you, hold you so tight,
making' love to ya, baby, all through the night.
Nibble on your ear, taste your lips,

making magic, girl, as I squeeze your hips.
Let your hair fall all around me, don't care if you tease.
Cause, baby, it's you that I'm out to please.

RAP

Well, I gotta little something I need to tell you.
There's a few ideas that I wanna follow through.
Wanna hold ya tight, tell ya that I love ya,
kiss on ya shoulders as I lie above ya.
Wanna work down down to da bottom.
What's dat look? Don't tell me that I'm rotten.
Just a little sneaky, but on the sweet side.
Come on, roll over. Let your hips glide.
Kiss on my chest, scratch on my back.
just a little rough. I like it like dat.
But as I rub your body, gentle and smooth,
I just wanna please ya. That's all I gotta prove.

CHORUS

Let me caress you, hold you so tight,
making' love to ya, baby, all through the night.
Nibble on your ear, taste your lips,
making magic, girl, as I squeeze your hips.
Let your hair fall all around me, don't care if you tease.
Cause, baby, it's you that I'm out to please.

Cause, baby, it's you I'm out to please.

JULY 21, 1993

I'm Yours

VERSE I
Wanting you with every breath
with every sigh,
The sparkle in your eye.

And to touch you, it's a miracle.
It's unbelievable.
You're so wonderful.

CHORUS
All I know.
All I am.
Just a man.
Take my hand.
Walk with me.
Through all the doors.
Baby, if you're sure,
I'm yours.

VERSE II
Watching you by candlelight
On a winter's night.
Oh, how this feels so right.

Oh this feeling I can't resist.
The moment that we kissed
Must have started this.

CHORUS
All I know.
All I am.

Just a man.
Take my hand.
Walk with me.
Through all the doors.
Baby, if you're sure,
I'm yours.

BRIDGE
I'm yours till you're finished.
I'm yours till you're through.
I'm yours as long as you want me.
Baby, I belong to you.

MUSICAL BRIDGE

CHORUS
All I know.
All I am.
Just a man.
Take my hand.
Walk with me.
Through all the doors.
Baby, if you're sure,
I'm yours.

1/6/95

WE'RE GONNA BE ALRIGHT

VERSE I

The thought of you leavin', girl,
Slowly takes over my mind…
But I'm never gonna let you go.
You were much too hard to find.

We're gonna work through this,
No matter how far apart.
You will always be here with me, baby,
hangin' round my heart.

CHORUS

We're gonna be alright
Cause I'm so in love, girl.
And you're so much a part of my life.
We're gonna be alright.
Right here waiting to hold you,
Hold you close and tight.
We're gonna be alright.
We're gonna be alright.

VERSE II

I can't imagine not havin' you here each day,
But my love will keep you warm, baby,
All the time you're away.

I wish I could be there with you,
Holdin' you so close and tight.
Just remember that I love you,
And think of me all through the night.

CHORUS
We're gonna be alright
Cause I'm so in love, girl,
And you're so much a part of my life.
We're gonna be alright.
Right here waiting to hold you,
Hold you close and tight.
We're gonna be alright.
We're gonna be alright.

BRIDGE
We're gonna make it.
I swear, baby. I swear.
You won't be gone forever,
But forever is what we'll share.

CHORUS
We're gonna be alright
Cause I'm so in love, girl,
And you're so much a part of my life.
We're gonna be alright.
Right here waiting to hold you,
Hold you close and tight.
We're gonna be alright.
We're gonna be alright.

8/22/93

You Chose Me

Well, I know
you could have had it all.
And I know
you deserve it all.

You could have all the things that money buys
without spending a dime.
Men would lay the world at your feet
for a minute of your time.

Sometimes, I feel worthless,
and I can't see.
Why?
You chose me.

Well, I know
I ain't got much at all.
And I know
you don't want it all.

But I will give you all the things
that money cannot buy.
I will lay my heart down at your feet.
I will give you my life.

I feel so lucky,
and you don't know how much it means.
That
you chose me.

I don't know why and I still can't see.
But I thank you.
'Cause?
You chose me.

You chose me.

10/97

When We Get There

VERSE I
Big white house, picket fence.
We host big parties on the weekends.
I write songs. You take care of the kids.
If this ain't heaven, I don't know what is.

CHORUS
We've come so far, but, Honey, not far enough.
We ain't got much, but we got a lot of love.
That perfect life is what we'll share.
I can't wait till we get there...

AHHH AHHH AHHH When we get there.

VERSE II
3 bedroom trailer, beat up truck.
We work too hard to depend on luck.
We both have jobs and want a few kids.
If this ain't heaven, I don't know what is.

CHORUS
We've come so far, but, Honey, not far enough.
We ain't got much, but we got a lot of love.
That perfect life is what we'll share.
I can't wait till we get there....

AHHH AHHH AHHH When we get there.

(Guitar Solo)

BRIDGE
I know, Darlin›, it›s a whole lot of dreams.

Sometimes our life is hard as it seems.
Baby, can you smell it? That fresh clean air
blowin' off the beach, when we get there.

CHORUS
We've come so far, but, Honey, not far enough.
We ain't got much, but we got a lot of love.
That perfect life is what we'll share.
I can't wait till we get there…

AHHH AHHH AHHH When we get there.

Yeah, when we get there.
When we get there.

2001

What Love Really Means

Verse I

It was snowin' that night on the way down 75.
The wipers were frozen, and I could barely see to drive.
When I looked at you, you were sound asleep
In a U-Haul truck southbound for Tennessee.

(soft music)

I could feel your dreams as if they were my own.
In the fast lane headed for our new home
Not even a map just a pocket full of dreams,
Searchin' for what love really means.

Chorus

Holdin' you close in the winter snow,
whispering softly I'll never let go,
holdin' your hand as we chase all our dreams,
fueled by the desire of what love really means.
Keep holdin' onto what love really means.

Verse II

When you're 71 and I'm 75,
when my hair turns gray, and I can barely see to drive,
I'll look at you as you lay fast asleep
on a big old' mountain somewhere in Tennessee.

I can feel your dreams because they are my own.
You're in my heart, my soul, my mind. You're in my bones.
Things may not always work out like we plan,
but we'll keep searching for what love means, hand in hand.

CHORUS
Holdin' you close in the winter snow,
whispering softly I'll never let go,
holdin' your hand as we chase all our dreams,
fueled by the desire of what love really means.
Keep holdin' onto what love really means.

12/05/01

You're All I Need To Find

Verse I

I've been lost now for quite some time,
Goin' round and round in a circle.
Seems I'm losing my mind.
I've tried north. I've tried south,
East and west.
Just left a bad taste in my mouth.
I bought a map, but it gave me no clue.
It had directions for everywhere,
But it didn't point to you.

Chorus

And you're all I need to find.
No matter where you're hidden.
In a kingdom that's forbidden,
I'll do anything I have to do
Just to get to you.
When I find the path that's mine,
You'll be there
'Cause you're all I need to find.

Verse II

You may be near. You may be far,
But I can see your eyes
In every shining star.
I would walk to the moon
Or stare at the sun until I'm blind
To see if you are there
'Cause you're all I need to find.

Chorus II
You're all I need to find,
All that I'm looking for.
I'll open each and every door,
Just to peek inside
For just one reason why.
You are all I need to find.

Break
I'd hop a train, but a plan would be faster,
Steal a Cadillac, try it horseback.
There's nothing I wouldn't do,
Just to get to you.

Chorus III
'Cause you are all I need to find,
To hold together the pieces of my mind.
No matter what the cost, I'll forever be lost.
Just one thing can make me fine.
It's not a sunken treasure. I only seek one pleasure.
You're all I need to find.

I'll search till the end of time
'Cause you're all I need to find.

2/10/11

The Wizard of Love

Verse I

You make such a twisted mind
seem so simple.
You make such a twisted mind
go insane.
You make such a twisted mind
seem a little more straight, girl.
Um-huh-uh-umm
You make the crazy man
all heart, no needless brain.

Chorus I

Baby, can you keep on doin'
What you're doin'?
Puttin' back together
this ol' scarecrow,
Holdin' my hand forever.
I'll keep on keepin' on
down your yellow brick road.

Verse II

You make such a broken heart
beat again.
You make such a broken heart
feel whole.
You make such a broken heart
guide me, girl.
Um-hum-uh-um
You make this tin man
squeak free and gold.

Chorus II

Baby, can you keep on doin'
what you're doin'?
Givin' CPR
To this old tin man,
my heart in your hands forever.
I'll keep on keepin' on
down your yellow brick road.

Bridge

I don't really know where I'm going.
I don't really care.
But I have to do something.
These flying monkeys are everywhere.

Verse III

I've been so scared
my whole life through.
I've been so scared,
no courage to find.
I've been so scared,
but now the fear is fading, girl.
Um-hum, uh-hum
You make this cowardly cat
A fearless, raging lion.

Chorus III

Baby, can you keep on doin'
what you're doin'?
Putting courage in the cowardly lion.
I'll roar and protect you forever
as I keep on keepin' on
down your yellow brick road.

CLOSING

The wicked witch has no chance
as we go farther,
wearing your ruby red slippers.
Douse the bitch with water.

1/14/14

It's Time I Lay My Burdens Down

Chorus
I always walked a fine line
between right and wrong
from the words in the poems
and the way I lived my songs.
Don't get confused between who I was then
And who I am now.
Death comes for them all
It's time I lay my burdens down.

Verse I
I don't wanna be who I am.
Could you tell when I darkened your door?
I'm gonna lay down my cards.
Can I cross them on my floor?
It will just take a minute.
Can I light a candle in here?
Please forestall your judgment.
Set aside your fear.

Chorus
I always walked a fine line
between right and wrong
from the words in the poems
and the way I lived my songs.
Don't get confused between who I was then
And who I am now.
Death comes for them all
It's time I lay my burdens down.

Verse II

I will not avoid authorities.
I'm gonna slay all the judges if I get the votes.
I will sail around the world
If I can get through the Cape of Good Hope.
Believe in me.
Summon the courage if you can.
Fuck you and your doubts, so goes the son of man.

Chorus

I always walked a fine line
between right and wrong
from the words in the poems
and the way I lived my songs.
Don't get confused between who I was then
And who I am now.
Death comes for them all
It's time I lay my burdens down.

Bridge/End

Spread my wings and fly.
Spread my wings and cry.
I will never see Heaven
if I never die,
crumble to the ground.
It's time to lay my burdens down.

3/31/14

Sometimes It Hurts

VERSE I
I like to say
that I lost it all.
But who's to say
I don't have farther to fall.

It's an endless trip
from the bottom to the top
and back again
when you crash into the rocks.

CHORUS I
And it hurts
when you feel you've lost everything.
And it hurts
to watch your best friend die at seventeen.
And it hurts
when it seems all your dreams just fall apart.
And it hurts
when there's nowhere left to start.

VERSE II
I should have died
a number of times.
But I guess the Lord
must be a friend of mine.

My arm ain't much use.
My kidneys are shot.
My liver is gone
from all the abuse it got.

CHORUS II

And it hurts
knowing you pissed it all away.
And it hurts
just to carry on another day.
And it hurts
living without the ones you've lost.
And it hurts
when you can't afford the cost.

BREAK

Oh please, oh please take this hurt from me.
Let me have just one more good day to see.
I simply don't know how much more I can take.
Please God, no more baggage, my soul's about to break.

VERSE III

Even my spirit is gone.
I feel so old.
I had everything,
wasn't much, truth be told.

It was all I wanted,
an old rock house and a broke down car,
the perfect job,
singing in honky-tonk bars.

CHORUS III

And it hurts
to feel it slip away.
And it hurts
to watch your hair turn to gray.
And it hurts
when you run out of luck.

And it hurts
to just give up.

Break II/Ending
And when the tears fill your eyes,
just let'em fly.
Don't be afraid to cry
'cause sometimes it hurts.
Yeah, sometimes it hurts.

8/27/11

Place To Die

(CHORUS)
Everybody needs a place to die...
a little place to find some peace and quiet.
Get down low or rest up on high.
I'm just looking for my place to die.

(VERSE I)
Rest my bones 'neath a willow tree.
But there won't be no weeping there for me.
A shady spot to call my own...
... where I can sit and wait for my call home.

(CHORUS)
Everybody needs a place to die...
...a little place to find some peace and quiet.
Get down low or rest up on high.
I'm just looking for my place to die.

(VERSE II)
Lay out a mossy old rock for my headstone.
Inscribe that a man here died alone.
Make no mistake, don't bury me;
I want to be burned so my soul flies free.

(CHORUS)
Everybody needs a place to die...
... a little place to find some peace and quiet.
Get down low or rest up on high.
I'm just looking for my place to die.

(BRIDGE)
Sooner than later, the reaper will show.
Will he be surprised that I'm
ready to go?
No begging. No pleading.
No tears I'll cry.
I'm just looking for my place to die.

(CHORUS)
Everybody needs a place to die...
... a little place to find some peace and quiet.
Get down low or rest up on high.
I'm just looking for my place to die.

(VERSE III)
I won't run. I won't hide.
I'm just looking for my place to die.
I don't know how, but I know it's time.
So I reckon this'll do for my place to die.

I am ready and it's my time.
I'll lie right here in my place to die.

11/24/11

Plastic Flowers

Verse I

On this crooked old road
that leads me in and out of here,
a lot of folks are driving fast,
driving without fear.
Around every mountain curve lies a memory
of someone's last ride
and a friend that used to be.

Chorus I

So I don't need no plastic flowers on the highway
to remind me that she's passed away.
Didn't make the curve.
Fell asleep.
Or lost her nerve.
Or simply someone else's mistake.
So damn them plastic flowers on the highway.

Verse II

They hold so many stories,
but they can't really talk.
Every time I pass one,
it makes me wanna walk.
I get so very angry at this God forsaken place.
There just ain't no way
they could've made this narrow road straight.

Chorus II

But I don't need no plastic flowers on the highway
To remind me of her last day.
A little too much to drink.

On the phone.
Or just a blink.
There just ain't no way to say…
So damn them plastic flowers on the highway.

BRIDGE
I just went past it.
The wood cross
and the damned cheap plastic
flowers on the highway.

CHORUS III
I don't need no plastic flowers on the highway.
They ain't really got nothing to say.
Please take'em down.
I know she's in the ground,
every time I go around that way.
Damn them plastic flowers on the highway.
Plastic flowers on the highway.

ENDING
Around every mountain curve lies a memory
of someone's last ride
and a friend that used to be.

10/1/11

OLD BROWN HOUSE

VERSE I

I can›t find that old brown house
you're looking for.
I looked in all the places
it should've been.
It almost makes a man like me
feel like a failure.
Tomorrow is a brand new day
and I'll try again.
Because to me
that's what it means to be a friend.

CHORUS I

Rain or shine,
a stormy sky.
I won't let your memories die.
If that little brown house
still stands,
I'll be the man who finds it.
I'll ask everyone
under the sun
if they even know the one.
I'll pray tonight for a guiding light
to help me find the way
down the right road
I have to go
to find that old brown house.

VERSE II

I still ain›t had no luck
to speak of.

Lord, I hope it still stands,
and it ain't been painted,
at least, any other color than brown.
My truck hit empty,
'bout an hour ago.
But as long as I can walk,
I'll hunt it down.

Chorus I
Rain or shine,
a stormy sky.
I won't let your memories die.
If that little brown house
still stands,
I'll be the man who finds it.
I'll ask everyone
under the sun
if they even know the one.
I'll pray tonight for a guiding light
to help me find the way
down the right road.
I have to go
to find that old brown house.

(electric guitar solo)
(heavy piano)

Bridge
That old brown house
has hid from me.
But we can sit under the shade of a tree,
you can explain it to me,
what it's all about,
and I will work the lyrics out.

Richard Corey 290

And then you won't forget about
the memory of that old brown house.

Chorus II
Rain or shine,
your house or mine,
I won't let your memories die.
Tell me how it sounds,
how it swings,
and I'll buy me a new 3rd string.
We'll drink some of my homemade wine,
bourbon, or some good moonshine.
I'll find the way
to what I need to say
to help you find that old brown house.
We'll find that old brown house.

4/14/14

Tragic Comedy

Verse I
Life twists and turns.
It hollows as it burns
into your soul.

Dreams come and go.
Your fate will flow
until you're buried
in a six foot hole.

Chorus I
But life is beautiful,
you see.
The flowers and the grass and the trees.
But who's to say I have ever been free
or just the main character
in a tragic comedy?

Verse II
Near or far,
wherever you are,
I hope you're fine.

Upon the moon and stars,
Milky Way or Mars,
You're on my mind.

Chorus II
Life is wonderful, you know,
like the sun's eternal glow.
But who's to say

it's all free for me,
the main character
in a tragic comedy.

LA-LA LA-LA LA-LA
LA-LA LA-LA LA-LA
When did it all begin,
and how's a tragic comedy to end?

(MUSICAL BREAK)

VERSE III
I take a breath and sigh
as the curtains rise
in the night

waiting to cross
before I get lost
in the light.

CHORUS III
Life is magical, for real.
Depending on how you feel.
But who decides what it's gonna be
when you're the main character
of a tragic comedy.

LA-LA LA-LA LA-LA
LA-LA LA-LA LA-LA

FINALE
We all should take a break
and leave the tragic comedy
up to fate.

A tragic comedy
covered in age.
Another tragic comedy,
turn the page.

3/10/08

Everybody Needs a Place to Die

Verse I

I'm on my way back home.
I've gotta find a place to lie.
'Cause everybody needs a place to die.
Everybody needs a place to die.

Verse II

I hope that no one's at home.
I wanna be alone.
I've gotta shed my bones.
On the ground I'll lie,
'cause everybody needs a place to die.
Everybody needs a place to die.

Chorus I

Everybody needs a place to die.
Some choose to be in the long tall pines.
Others choose the sweet sunshine.
Many don't care where people might find
their bodies and where they lie.
If I don't make it home tonight,
I'll find a beautiful place to lie.
'Cause everybody needs a place to die.
Everybody needs a place to lie.

Verse III

I don't need a nice tombstone
or a funny box to hold my bones.
No hard work, just a handful of dirt,
and that is where I'll lie.

'Cause everybody needs a place to die.
Everybody needs a place to die.

VERSE IV
A grassy field or underneath a tree
that would be just fine by me.
Or burn my bones to set me free,
And in the ashes, I will lie.
'Cause everybody needs a place to die.
Everybody needs a place to die.

CHORUS II
Everybody needs a place to die.
Look the devil straight in the eye
but on to Heaven I will fly.
In the face of God, I will cry.
I won't ask for any more time,
'cause I only need a place to die.
Everybody needs a place to die.
Everybody needs a place to die.

6/22/14

A Prayer for Me

Hey, Old Man, I ain't done this in a while,
but I'm getting tired
and I've forgotten how to smile.
So if you could spare the time,
I really wish you would.
It's about time that things went from bad to good.

I'm not quite sure how to do it right.
So I guess this is a prayer for me.
I ain't as close to You or Jesus as I need to be.
All I ask for is a little off my load
'cause my shoulders are tired and my back is bowed.
Can I please have a shot at eternity?
I am sorry for the man I turned out to be.

I know I started out strong and fast when I was young.
I was naive, foolish, headstrong, and dumb.
I know You have helped me out from time to time,
but look at me now, Lord, my light has ceased to shine.

I don't wanna mess this up,
so could You walk me through?
I have no explanation for the things I do.
So, Lord, this is a prayer just for me.
I'm just lookin' for a shot
to live another couple days or three.
All I got are these words

that I'm too tired to speak.
I'm sorry, Lord, for the man I turned out to be.

(Guitar Solo)

(Piano Solo)

Hey, Old Man, what You got to say?
I ain't walked the straight and narrow.
I guess I lost my way.

I must be close to Hell
'cause my feet are hot.
Could you have an angel start pullin' up with all he's got.

I'm gonna use my last breath
to say a prayer for me.
I'm sorry, Lord, for the man I turned out to be.

(Sighs)... funny.

4/15/11

The World Is Still Mine

Verse I

People say I can't do this shit no more.
Can I do it if I do it on a foreign shore?
Where they don't know me.
Don't know that I'm country.
Would the kids' car stereos wanna pump me?
A big drum loop,
That bumps like Toucan Sam snortin' FruitLoops.
You'll never see me commercially
On your TV
Unless it's marketed for your parents.
I'm so damn old I'm fuckin' transparent.
You can see through me.
But you can't see in me.
I gotta blinding passion for vocabulary.
That's what's in me.
It's in my blood.
It's in my brain.
My Grandpa's blues have made me go insane.
I'm gonna get my ass up in the morning
"I'll believe I'll dust my broom."
Sweep out a path in front of my door,
Even though I don't use the motherfucker no more.
I'm trapped in the woods.
I'll never get my message out,
No matter how loud my country ass can shout.
It wouldn't matter any way.
I ain't no G no more.
Just an OG that hangs out in front of the liquor store.
That's right. My right arm is half gone.
But so are the motherfuckers that took it,

I did it all on my own.
Fear is a bitch if you got any.
Lucky for me I ain't got many.
I ain't afraid to live. I ain't afraid to die.
I ain't afraid to put a motherfucking pencil through your eye.
You can't threaten me.
I'm the threat and I live in the trees.
In a place way beyond the pines,
Back in the woods and the fuckin' world is still mine.

(LOOP)
In the pines, in the pines, where the sun don't ever shine,
I will shiver the whole night through.
My girl, my girl, where will you go, I am goin' where the cold wind blows.
In the pines, in the pines, where the sun don't ever shine. I will shiver the whole night through.

VERSE II
You can't fuck with me bitch 'cause I've been to the crossroads and made my deal.
All you got left to do, little piggy, is squeal.
I'll step to the mic with my fuckin' boots on,
Everybody thinking I am gonna sing a country song,
But the devil comes out of my mouth like a rattlesnake.
Bass from the speakers causing the whole fucking place to shake.
And it's my spit, my shit, my hit. Straight to the top,
While all you other motherfuckers just sitting there with your mouths dropped.
Bit by my poison. Hit with my rock.
You never know exactly how I'm gonna flow.
Fast as a Lamborghini or I can roll real slow,
Like a drive by on a fucking buck deer,
Because they ain't no fucking people out here.

I'm a thousand miles from nowhere
And that's exactly where I need to be
To keep the world safe.
Because the fucking world still belongs to me.

(Loop)
In the pines, in the pines, where the sun don't ever shine,
I will shiver the whole night through.
My girl, my girl, where will you go, I am goin' where the cold wind
blows.
In the pines, in the pines, where the sun don't ever shine. I will
shiver the whole night through.

Verse III
Poor old worthless me is the only friend I ever made.
Maybe 'cause the other motherfuckers were afraid
And no one could find where I stayed.
I'd slither out of the woods to wind up a lucky woman's leg.
A different one every night to keep the Lizard King satisfied.
Won't be long till I lay down and die.
But ain't no bitch gonna rub me out.
I'm just gonna drift off to dream and never come out.
Pour myself a glass of sangria,
Do a little Santeria,
Drink a little blood,
Pour a little on the ground.
The world is mine and after death I'll still wear the fucking crown.

(Loop)
In the pines, in the pines, where the sun don't ever shine,
I will shiver the whole night through.

My girl, my girl, where will you go, I am goin' where the cold wind blows.
In the pines, in the pines, where the sun don't ever shine. I will shiver the whole night through.

The world is mine. The world is mine.
Deep Deep Deep in the Pines.

6/7/14

WRITTEN BY: RICHARD COREY

9/5/14

Printed in the United States
By Bookmasters